# Mental Chaos

Mental Help In The Mental Cloud

**Corey Herriman**

# Contents

# Introduction

In today's world, constant online connection is the norm. We scroll through feeds, jumping from platform to platform, feeling more connected globally than ever before. Ironically, this digital age has also led to increased feelings of isolation, information overload, and a deep longing for genuine human connection. We seek to know more, yet often feel less understood, especially when it comes to navigating the complexities of mental health.

My name is Corey Herriman. At first glance, you might see me as just another 36-year-old guy passionate about real estate who finds joy in a great game of golf, thrills at the challenge of motocross, and loves nothing more than being outdoors. However, there's more to me. My daily life involves a personal battle with mental health, not just as a concept, but as a lived experience. This journey has given me a unique perspective that I'm passionate about sharing.

"Mental Chaos: Mental Help In The Mental Cloud" was born from a desire to guide you through the often-confusing world of mental health discussions. It aims to bring clarity and equip you with tools to manage your well-being. By combining my personal experiences with the latest scientific research, this book acts as your compass in the complexities of mental health. My goal is to create a community where discussing mental health is not only accepted but actively encouraged.

Understanding mental health is no small feat, especially today. Recent studies underscore the critical nature of mental wellness, showing a significant rise in digital burnout and information overload—challenges that weren't as prevalent in previous generations. The importance of addressing mental health is urgent and cannot be overlooked with the seriousness it deserves.

I know you. You've felt the weight of too much information yet not enough understanding. You've faced the stigma of seeking help and felt the exhaustion of digital burnout. This book sees you and understands your struggles. This book acknowledges your struggles and aims to provide support. Through actionable strategies, personal stories, scientific insights, and even interactive elements like QR codes for additional resources, I invite you on a journey towards better mental health.

Let's approach this path with an open mind and a willingness to engage deeply with the exercises and reflections provided. Consider this book not just a resource but a companion equipped with warmth, humor, and a genuine desire to make a difference in your life.

As we embark on this journey together, I want to leave you with a personal note: I hope this book lights a path to guide you through your mental health journey. Know that you are not alone. Together, we can build a supportive community, breaking down the barriers that keep us isolated and misunderstood.

"Mental Chaos" is more than just a book; it's a unique toolkit designed specifically for you. It blends personal experience with scientific research and practical advice. With its interactive features and focus on community building, this book offers support every step of the way.

Let's begin this journey together, understanding that there are clear, practical, and effective guidelines to guide us through the vast and often intimidating cloud of mental health information.

# Chapter 1: Dailys

In today's digital age, we're constantly bombarded with information. From social media feeds to news alerts and everything in between, there's a relentless stream of content vying for our attention. This constant influx doesn't just strain our ability to process information (cognitive load), it can also significantly impact our mental well-being. Imagine standing under a powerful waterfall, desperately trying to catch water in your cupped hands. No matter how hard you squeeze, the sheer volume overwhelms you, and most of it inevitably spills through. This metaphor perfectly captures the dilemma of navigating mental health in today's information age. We're surrounded by a sea of data, struggling to identify what's truly relevant and helpful.

## 1.1 Navigating Mental Health in the Era of Information Overload

### The Challenge of Abundance

Today, we have access to a vast amount of mental health information online. There are countless articles, videos, and resources available, all aiming to provide guidance and support. While this abundance might seem like a positive development, it can often lead to confusion and even increased stress. This creates a paradox: resources intended to help can become overwhelming.

For example, someone seeking information on managing anxiety might find millions of search results. Each source may claim effectiveness, but conflicting advice can leave you feeling more anxious than before you started searching.

### Filtering Effectively

The internet is very vast and contains tons of information on mental health—some wanted and some unwanted. Articles, videos, and resources abound, promising guidance and support. However, this abundance can quickly become overwhelming and even counterproductive.

The key to navigating this deluge lies in developing a critical approach to information filtering. Think of yourself as a detective, carefully evaluating the source and content. Prioritize credible resources from established organizations like the World Health Organization or reputable medical institutions. Seek out information based on scientific research, ideally citing studies or expert opinions.

This process is akin to brewing a perfect cup of coffee. A good filter allows the rich, robust flavors to come through while removing the unwanted grounds. Similarly, a critical approach helps you sift through the information, extracting valuable insights and discarding the unreliable or irrelevant.

**The Role of Digital Literacy**

In today's digital age, navigating information overload is crucial when seeking mental health resources. Digital literacy, which goes beyond simply using technology, is a key tool. It's about understanding how to assess the information you encounter online.

For example, checking publication dates helps ensure the advice you're reading is current. Reliable websites often have clear information about the author, cite their sources. Recognizing these signs helps you identify high-quality content.

These digital literacy skills are essential additions to your mental health toolkit. By learning to navigate the online world effectively, you can find trustworthy information and manage your mental health with more confidence.

**Setting Boundaries**

The vast amount of mental health information online can be incredibly helpful, but it's important to find a balance. The digital world can easily become overwhelming if we're constantly plugged in.

One key strategy is learning when to step away. Setting boundaries could involve using a timer for internet use or scheduling specific times for checking social media. Just like limiting caffeine for a good night's sleep, limiting digital consumption can prevent information overload. This allows your mind to rest and process the information you've already absorbed.

Creating "digital-free zones" can be helpful. Try putting your phone away during meals, for the first hour after waking up, or before bed. This allows for direct engagement with the world around you and reduces the feeling of being overwhelmed. Taking breaks from screens improves your ability to process and apply the information you've learned.

In today's information age, the challenge lies not just in accessing information, but in selecting, processing, and using it wisely. Developing skills to filter effectively, boosting your digital literacy, and setting boundaries can transform mental health resources from a burden to a benefit. These strategies extend beyond mental health information. They can guide your approach to the entire digital world, leading to a more balanced, informed, and healthy life.

## 1.2 Analysis Paralysis: When Too Much Information Becomes a Barrier

The current digital age provides information that is seemingly limitless. Any question can be answered with a few taps on a screen. This should be empowering, especially when it comes to mental health resources. However, a surprising phenomenon often occurs.

The vast amount of mental health advice available online, instead of guiding us clearly, can leave us feeling lost in a sea of uncertainty.

This is known as analysis paralysis, a situation where the sheer volume of information actually hinders our ability to make decisions. The abundance of choices, ironically, can make taking the first step towards improving our mental health feel overwhelming.

**The Paralysis Phenomenon**

Imagine standing in the cereal aisle of a grocery store, faced with hundreds of options. You came in thinking you needed cereal, but deciding which one to pick has become overwhelming. This everyday scenario mirrors our experience with online mental health resources. The options seem endless, and the fear of making the wrong choice can lead to inaction. It's a paradox where having too many choices doesn't liberate us but confines us, leaving us standing still, unable to choose.

**Decision Fatigue**

The constant barrage of choices we face every day takes a toll on our mental resources. This phenomenon, called decision fatigue, describes how every decision we make, big or small, uses up some of our mental stamina. Just like our muscles get tired after exertion, our brains can become fatigued from making too many choices.

In the context of mental health, this can be a significant hurdle. When faced with a sea of treatment options or coping strategies, decision fatigue can make it feel overwhelming to choose a path forward. Our mental energy is limited, and the constant decisions we make throughout the day can deplete our reserves. This leaves us with less mental firepower to tackle the important choices that truly impact our well-being.

**Simplifying Choices**

The constant barrage of information and options online can lead to two problems: decision fatigue, where making too many choices drains our mental energy, and analysis paralysis, where the sheer volume of information makes it difficult to choose anything at all.

Combatting these hurdles requires a conscious effort to simplify our choices. This doesn't mean ignoring the wealth of information available, but rather approaching it strategically. The key is to focus on what truly matters to us.

Here are a few techniques to help narrow down the options and find the mental health resources that best suit your needs:

**Prioritize:** Determine what aspect of your mental health needs immediate attention and prioritize resources that address this issue.

**Limit your sources:** Choose a handful of trusted websites or authors and restrict your search to these. This reduces the temptation to veer off into the vastness of available information.

**Set a time limit:** Allocate a specific amount of time for research. Once this time is up, step away. This prevents endless searching and encourages you to make decisions based on the information you have.

**Seek recommendations:** Sometimes, the best way to simplify your search is to ask for recommendations from trusted individuals or professionals in the mental health field.

**Taking the First Step**

The key to overcoming analysis paralysis is often simply taking action, even if it's small. Starting can be a powerful antidote to feeling overwhelmed by options. Focus on making one change or trying a single technique at a time. This approach reduces the pressure to find the “perfect” solution and allows you to experiment and see what works best for you.

Remember, mental health is a personal journey. What works wonders for one person might not be effective for another. The goal is to find what resonates with you, and that may involve some trial and error.

For example, if managing stress is your top priority, begin with just one stress-reduction technique. Maybe it’s dedicating five minutes each day to deep breathing exercises. Consistency is key. By sticking to this one change, you can assess its impact on your well-being. If it works, fantastic! You’ve discovered a helpful tool. If not, you’ve gained valuable insight into what doesn’t work for you and can move on to try something else without feeling like you wasted time or energy.

By tackling analysis paralysis and decision fatigue, we’re not just navigating the sea of mental health information; we’re also developing valuable decision-making skills that benefit us in all aspects of life. Simplifying choices, setting clear priorities, and acting one step at a time empowers us to move forward on our mental health journey and in our daily lives.

## 1.3 The Double-Edged Sword of Social Media on Mental Wellness

Social media has become an undeniable thread woven into the fabric of our daily lives. It offers a complex mix of connection and isolation, impacting our mental health in significant ways. This multifaceted role of social media warrants a closer look, especially as we navigate the challenges of maintaining mental well-being in a hyper-connected world.

### The Connectivity Conundrum

Social media platforms, on the surface, promise endless opportunities for connection. We can stay in touch with loved ones across vast distances, share life's milestones, and discover communities built around shared interests. However, this very connectivity can come at a cost. The very tools designed to bring us closer can also amplify feelings of isolation. Scrolling through carefully curated feeds filled with others' highlights can leave us feeling strangely alone, despite being surrounded by a virtual crowd. This is a peculiar kind of loneliness, born from the contradiction of being connected to many yet having few truly intimate connections. Acknowledging this paradox is the first step towards mitigating its negative impact on our mental health.

**Comparative Despair**

Social media feeds are inherently prone to fostering a culture of comparison, tapping into our natural tendency to measure ourselves against others. Unfortunately, these comparisons often lead to feelings of despair rather than inspiration. Seeing snapshots of seemingly perfect lives, filled with success, beauty, and happiness can distort our perception of our own lives, overshadowing our personal achievements and joys. It's crucial to remember that social media is essentially a highlight reel, not a comprehensive documentary of someone's reality. Everyone faces challenges; they simply don't make it onto the feed as often. Breaking free from this cycle of comparison requires a conscious shift in focus towards our own unique journey. We must recognize that each person's path is different and cannot be fairly compared to the curated online presence of others.

**Positive Platforms**

Despite the challenges, there are encouraging developments in the way social media is being used to positively impact mental health. Many platforms and initiatives are dedicated to breaking down the stigma surrounding mental health issues, offering support networks, and sharing valuable resources. From online forums providing safe spaces to share personal stories to accounts offering daily affirmations and mental health tips, these positive online communities can be a source of comfort, understanding, and practical advice. They serve as a powerful reminder that we're not alone in our struggles, and engaging with them thoughtfully can be a valuable tool on our mental health journey.

**Personal Boundaries**

Protecting our mental well-being in the age of social media requires establishing clear personal boundaries. This might involve limiting the amount of time spent scrolling, actively curating our feeds to prioritize positive and supportive content, or taking regular digital detoxes. Here are some specific strategies to consider:

**Time Limits:** Utilize built-in app features or separate apps to monitor and limit social media usage. Setting specific times for checking social media can prevent it from consuming our day.

**Curating Your Feed:** Make a conscious effort to follow accounts that uplift and support your mental health. Unfollow or mute those that trigger negative feelings. This simple action can significantly transform your social media experience.

**Active Engagement:** Shift from passive scrolling to active participation. Comment on posts that resonate with you, share content that adds value, and use social media to foster genuine connections with others.

**Digital Detoxes:** Schedule regular breaks from social media entirely. These detox periods, whether a few hours daily or a complete weekend disconnect, can significantly benefit your mental health.

By implementing these boundaries, we can take control of our digital consumption and ensure that social media serves us, rather than detracts from, our overall well-being.

## 1.4 Digital Detox: Rediscovering Mental Peace Offline

In our constantly connected world, the concept of a digital detox has become more than just a trend; it's a vital tool for safeguarding our mental well-being. This section explores why taking intentional breaks from our devices can refresh our minds, how to effectively implement these detoxes, and the significant impact they can have on our mental health.

The constant barrage of notifications, pings, and the endless allure of scrolling have made our digital devices practically extensions of ourselves. However, this constant connectivity comes at a price: our mental peace. The constant hum of the digital world can drown out the quiet reflection and real-world engagement essential for our mental well-being. Recognizing the need for periodic disconnection isn't about abandoning technology altogether; it's about establishing a healthier relationship with it.

Putting a digital detox into practice requires more than just good intentions; it requires actionable steps. Start small by setting specific times of the day as tech-free zones. Mealtimes or the hour before bed are good places to begin. These designated windows can become pockets of calm, free from the demands of the digital world. As you progress, you can gradually build up to full-day detoxes, perhaps on weekends or during vacations. These breaks allow you to shift your focus from what's happening online to what's unfolding around you.

Reconnecting with the physical world doesn't necessitate grand adventures or elaborate plans. It can be as simple as taking a walk and truly noticing the details of your surroundings - the texture of the trees, the chirping of birds, or the rhythm of your own footsteps. Engaging in analog activities like reading a physical book, journaling by hand, or pursuing a craft can all ground you in the present moment, offering a welcome contrast to the constant screen glow.

One particularly effective practice for reinforcing the benefits of a digital detox is mindfulness. This could involve taking meditative walks, where each step is taken with intention and awareness, or practicing mindful eating, where you savor each bite without the distraction of screens. These practices not only enhance the detox experience but also cultivate a sense of presence that can permeate other areas of life, reducing the automatic urge to reach for your devices.

The stories of people who've successfully integrated digital detoxes into their lives serve as powerful testaments to the benefits of this practice. For instance, a writer discovered that disconnecting from the internet during mornings significantly boosted their productivity and creativity. Without the ability to browse or check emails, their mornings became prime time for focused, in-depth work. Another example is a busy parent who instituted weekend tech breaks for the entire family. This led to more quality time spent together, whether playing board games, exploring local parks, or simply having conversations. These stories all highlight a common thread: the discovery of a more balanced and enriched life when we create space between ourselves and our devices.

Digital detoxing isn't about demonizing technology; it's about cultivating a mindful approach to its use. We acknowledge that while our devices offer incredible benefits, they also have the potential to detract from our mental health if not managed wisely. By consciously disconnecting at times, we reclaim control over our attention and time, opening up space for activities and interactions that nourish our mental well-being.

This shift towards a more balanced digital life doesn't happen overnight. It requires patience, persistence, and a willingness to experiment to find what works best for you. But the rewards - improved mental clarity, reduced stress, and a deeper connection with the world around us - make the effort worthwhile.

## 1.5 The Rise of Teletherapy: Bridging the Gap or Widening It?

In recent years, teletherapy - the delivery of therapy sessions through video platforms - has witnessed a dramatic surge in popularity. This trend, accelerated by the global pandemic, has significantly transformed access to mental health services. However, it also presents new challenges and raises questions about the future of therapeutic relationships and care.

### Accessibility vs. Authenticity

The digital format of teletherapy has made mental healthcare more accessible for many who previously faced hurdles with traditional in-person therapy. Geographical limitations, time constraints, and even the stigma associated with attending physical therapy sessions are reduced when people can access care from the comfort and privacy of their own homes. However, this convenience raises questions about the authenticity of the connection between therapist and client. Can the depth of understanding and empathy established in a physical space be fully replicated through a screen?

Critics argue that subtle nonverbal cues, crucial for building a strong therapist-client relationship, can be missed during online sessions. Proponents counter this with research suggesting that many clients feel more at ease and open in the digital space, potentially leading to a different but equally valid connection.

### Personal Connection

Forming a therapeutic relationship online is certainly different from traditional settings. Some clients find the digital medium offers a sense of security, allowing them to share more freely. The screen acts as a buffer, reducing the feeling of vulnerability they might experience sitting face-to-face with a therapist. However, therapists must adapt their approach to foster connection without the benefit of physical presence. This may involve being more expressive verbally and through gestures to compensate for the lack of physical closeness. Maintaining eye contact and demonstrating active listening are also crucial despite the digital barrier.

**Technological Barriers**

While teletherapy has expanded access, it also highlights the existing digital divide. Not everyone has access to the necessary technology or reliable internet service, particularly in rural or underserved communities. This disparity creates a situation where those who could potentially benefit most from the accessibility of teletherapy are also the most likely to be excluded.

Addressing this issue requires multifaceted solutions. These range from policy changes that improve infrastructure in underserved areas to the development of teletherapy options that require lower bandwidth. Additionally, some services are experimenting with teletherapy delivered via phone calls. While lacking the visual component, phone therapy can still offer significant therapeutic benefits.

**Future Trends**

Looking ahead, teletherapy is poised for continued evolution. As technology advances, so too will the tools available for remote therapy. Virtual reality (VR) presents exciting possibilities, particularly in exposure therapy for anxiety disorders or PTSD. Imagine a client with agoraphobia gradually being exposed to anxiety-provoking environments in the safety of a virtual space, guided by their therapist.

Artificial intelligence (AI) could also enhance teletherapy platforms. From providing real-time feedback to improve session quality to handling administrative tasks, AI could free up therapists' time to focus more on client care.

Another emerging trend is the hybrid model of care, which combines the best aspects of both in-person and digital therapy. This model acknowledges that while teletherapy offers unmatched accessibility, there are situations where face-to-face interaction is beneficial. A hybrid approach allows therapists and clients to tailor the therapeutic experience to best meet the client's needs at any given time. For example, initial sessions might be conducted in-person to establish a strong connection, with subsequent sessions moving online for convenience, with the flexibility to switch back as needed.

Ultimately, teletherapy represents more than just a shift in how therapy is delivered; it's a reimagining of the therapeutic landscape. It challenges traditional notions of what effective therapy looks like and who it can benefit, pushing the boundaries of accessibility and convenience. However, it also compels us to continuously innovate to ensure that the authenticity and depth of the therapeutic relationship are preserved, regardless of the medium used.

The conversation surrounding teletherapy's role in mental health care is ongoing and requires continued dialogue among mental health professionals, clients, and policymakers to navigate the complexities of digital therapy. What remains clear is the significant potential of teletherapy to revolutionize the accessibility and delivery of mental health services in the digital age. Its evolution will undoubtedly play a critical role in addressing the broader challenges of mental healthcare in our increasingly digital world.

### 1.6 Personal Stories of Digital Burnout and Recovery

In our constantly connected world, where being online is often equated with productivity, the threat of digital burnout looms large. This isn't a fictional state; it's a very real experience characterized by exhaustion, decreased efficiency, and a growing sense of disillusionment with the digital world itself. It affects countless individuals who find themselves caught in the constant hum of emails, social media updates, and virtual meetings.

**Real Experiences**

Consider the story of a marketing professional who, without realizing it, was spending more time staring at screens than sleeping. Their days blurred together - a relentless cycle of checking emails, managing social media, and attending online meetings - leaving little room for rest or reflection. The wake-up call came in the form of physical symptoms: headaches, eye strain, and a persistent feeling of fatigue. Recognizing these as signs of digital burnout, they took decisive action. Strict boundaries were set around work hours and digital consumption. Gradually, the fog of burnout began to lift, replaced by a renewed sense of energy and a newfound appreciation for time spent offline.

Another example is a college student who fell victim to the trap of comparing their real life to the carefully curated images they saw on social media. This constant social comparison fueled a decline in their mental well-being, leading to isolation and anxiety. The path to recovery involved a conscious decision to limit social media use and focus on activities that fostered genuine self-esteem, such as volunteering and physical fitness. Over time, the need to measure up to online personas faded, revealing a path to a more authentic and fulfilling life.

These stories illustrate the diverse ways digital burnout can manifest and the importance of recognizing the warning signs. They also offer a message of hope: recovery is possible through conscious effort and a shift in digital habits.

**Lessons Learned**

These stories, while unique, converge on several vital lessons:

**Recognize the signs:** Identifying the early symptoms of digital burnout is crucial. These can range from physical cues like eye strain and sleep disturbances to emotional signals such as irritability or detachment from digital interactions.

**Set clear boundaries:** Establishing limits on digital engagement – whether through designated offline hours or specific no-screen zones in your home – can provide much-needed respite for the mind.

**Seek fulfilling offline activities:** Engaging in hobbies or interests that don't involve screens can provide a break from digital consumption and enrich your life meaningfully.

### The Role of Community

The stories of recovery from digital burnout highlight the importance of both online and offline communities. The marketing professional found a sense of belonging and a healthy outlet for stress by joining a local hobby group. In the real world, connecting with others who shared similar interests provided a much-needed escape from the digital world.

The student, on the other hand, discovered solace in online forums. Connecting with others who were struggling with social media comparison fostered a sense of solidarity and understanding. These experiences demonstrate the double-edged sword of digital platforms: while they can contribute to burnout, they can also offer valuable support networks. The key is to be mindful of how you engage with these spaces, prioritizing interactions that uplift and support your well-being.

### Strategies for Resilience

Building resilience against digital burnout requires both proactive and reactive measures. Here are some strategies inspired by real-life recoveries:

**Mindful engagement:** Before logging on, ask yourself what your intention is. This simple act of mindfulness can help steer your digital interactions towards more positive and purposeful engagement.

**Digital detoxes:** Regularly scheduled breaks from digital devices can help reset your relationship with technology, reducing reliance and mitigating the risk of burnout.

**Physical activity:** Incorporating regular exercise into your routine can offset some physical consequences of prolonged screen time, such as poor posture and reduced circulation, while also boosting mood and energy levels.

**Community involvement:** Whether online or in person, connecting with communities that share your interests or values can counterbalance the more superficial interactions that often dominate social media platforms.

Incorporating these strategies into daily life doesn't just offer a buffer against digital burnout and opens up a broader spectrum of experiences and connections, enriching our lives beyond the screen.

As we navigate the complexities of a digitally saturated world, these personal stories and the lessons they offer stand as beacons, guiding us toward a more balanced, healthy engagement with the digital realms. They remind us that, despite the challenges, recovery is possible, and often, it's the most superficial changes that can lead to the most profound improvements in our well-being.

## 1.7 The Science Behind Screen Time and Mental Health

Our digital devices connect us to a vast world of information and interaction, but they also come with potential downsides, especially when it comes to mental and physical health. The evidence is clear: excessive screen time can lead to significant changes in the brain, affecting everything from focus to sleep. Understanding these effects is crucial for developing healthy digital habits.

## Neurological Impacts

Neuroscience research is revealing how prolonged screen exposure can alter brain structure and function. Studies suggest a link between excessive screen time and reduced thickness in the prefrontal cortex, a region crucial for complex thinking, decision-making, and self-control. This thinning mirrors a decline in cognitive performance, hinting that our digital habits could reshape our brains and potentially impact our mental abilities.

Furthermore, the blue light emitted by screens disrupts our sleep-wake cycle, known as the circadian rhythm. This disruption makes it harder to fall asleep and stay asleep, impacting the quality of rest and leading to a range of mental health issues, from anxiety to depression.

## Physical Health Intersections

The conversation around screen time often focuses on mental health, but the physical consequences are equally important and closely linked. Extended screen use often leads to a more sedentary lifestyle, which is associated with various health problems like obesity, heart disease, and type 2 diabetes. These conditions, in turn, can worsen mental health, creating a cycle of decline that's difficult to break.

Eye strain, also called computer vision syndrome, is another physical consequence of screen time. Symptoms like dryness, blurred vision, and headaches can contribute to stress and decreased productivity, further affecting mental well-being.

## Age-specific Effects

The impact of screen time varies by age group, with children and adolescents being particularly vulnerable. Young brains are still developing and therefore more susceptible to external influences, including digital media. Excessive screen time in children has been linked to developmental delays, behavioral issues, and difficulties in school. Teenagers face additional risks, including cyberbullying, sleep problems, and distorted self-esteem due to the curated realities often presented on social media.

Adults are not immune to the negative effects of screen time, although the consequences may differ. In adults, excessive screen use is often associated with decreased well-being, increased loneliness, and a disrupted work-life balance, which can lead to burnout and strained relationships.

The key takeaway is that a balanced approach is essential. By understanding the science behind the impact of screens on our health, we can make informed choices about our digital habits and prioritize activities that promote both physical and mental well-being.

**Creating Healthy Habits**

In light of these findings, a mindful approach to screen use is imperative. Here are science-backed strategies designed to mitigate the negative impacts of screen time:

**Scheduled Breaks:** Implement the 20-20-20 rule to combat eye strain. Every 20 minutes, shift your gaze to something 20 feet away for at least 20 seconds. This brief pause can also be a mental reset, reducing cognitive fatigue.

**Tech-Free Zones:** Designate areas in your home, such as the bedroom or dining area, as tech-free zones. This helps reduce screen time and encourages healthier sleep hygiene and more meaningful family interactions.

**Mindful Consumption:** Engage with digital content intentionally. Ask yourself whether the content contributes positively to your day or serves a practical purpose. If not, it might be worth skipping.

**Physical Activity:** Counteract the sedentary lifestyle associated with screen use by integrating regular physical activity into your day—

even short walks or standing while on the phone can make a difference.

**Digital Curfews:** Set a cut-off time for screen use each evening to ensure screens don't interfere with your sleep. Aim to disconnect at least an hour before bedtime, creating a calming pre-sleep routine that doesn't involve screens.

**Quality Over Quantity:** When it comes to children and adolescents, focus on the quality of screen time rather than just the quantity. Educational content or video calls with family members can have a positive impact, promoting learning and connection.

Integrating these habits into our daily routines allows us to forge a healthier relationship with our digital devices. It's about finding a balance that allows us to reap the benefits of technology without falling prey to its pitfalls. The goal isn't to eliminate screen time but to create a mindful framework within which we can utilize technology as a tool for enhancement rather than a source of detriment to our mental and physical health.

### 1.8 Crafting Your Digital Mental Health Toolkit

In today's world, our digital devices can be a double-edged sword. They bombard us with a constant stream of information, fuel social comparison, and blur the lines between work and personal life, all of which can contribute significantly to stress. However, these same devices can also be powerful tools for managing stress. Meditation apps can guide us towards inner peace, mindfulness exercises can help us stay present in the moment, and connecting with loved ones online can provide invaluable social support. The key lies in creating a personalized digital mental health toolkit, a curated set of resources readily available at your fingertips, designed to address your unique needs and empower you to take charge of your mental well-being.

### Essential Apps and Resources

The first step in building this toolkit is curating a list of vetted digital tools that support mental health. This list can include:

**Meditation and Mindfulness Apps:** Tools like Headspace or Calm offer guided meditations to help reduce anxiety and improve sleep.

**Mood Tracking Apps:** Dailyo or Moodpath allows you to track your mood and mental health patterns over time, helping you identify triggers or trends.

**Cognitive Behavioral Therapy (CBT) Apps:** Platforms such as Woebot use AI to provide CBT techniques, offering support through conversational interfaces.

**Fitness Apps:** Given the vital link between physical and mental health, including a fitness app like Nike Training Club or YogaGlo can be beneficial.

It's important to remember that not all apps will resonate with everyone. Part of the process is trying different tools to see which align best with your needs and preferences.

### Customization Tips

Personalizing your digital toolkit is vital to making it a practical part of your mental health strategy. Here are some customization tips:

**Reflect on Your Needs:** Are you looking to manage anxiety, improve sleep, or boost your mood? Identifying your primary goals will help you select the most relevant tools.

**Test and Evaluate:** Spend a week or two with an app to see if it's helpful. It's okay to discard tools that don't feel right and keep looking for better fits.

**Combine Tools for Comprehensive Support:** Consider having a range of apps that support your mental health, from meditation to fitness to mood tracking.

### Integrating Tools into Daily Life

To make the most of these digital resources, integrating them into your daily routine is crucial. Here are some strategies:

**Set Reminders:** Use your phone or app reminders to prompt you to meditate, track your mood, or exercise. Consistency is vital to seeing benefits.

**Create Rituals:** Tie your mental health app usage to specific times of the day. For example, you are starting the day with a meditation session or ending it by filling in a mood tracker.

**Use Widgets:** Many smartphones allow you to add widgets to your home screen. Placing your mental health apps here can make them more accessible and top of mind.

### Staying Updated

The digital landscape constantly evolves, with new mental health tools being developed regularly. Here are some ways to keep your toolkit current:

**Follow Mental Health Advocates:** Many advocates on social media share the latest in digital mental health resources. Following a few trusted voices can keep you informed.

**Subscribe to Newsletters:** Numerous mental health newsletters review and recommend apps and digital tools.

**Regularly Review Your Toolkit:** Take stock of your digital toolkit every few months. Discard apps you no longer use and look for new ones offering additional benefits.

Creating and maintaining a digital mental health toolkit involves trial, personal reflection, and adjustment. The goal is to have a set of tools at your fingertips that you can rely on to support your mental well-being in this digital age.

## 1.9 Overcoming the Stigma in Cyberspace

The internet, a vast space for sharing ideas and sparking debate, can also be a breeding ground for a surprising phenomenon: the stigma around mental health. Despite progress in understanding these challenges, online spaces often mirror and amplify the prejudices we see in the real world. Recognizing how stigma manifests online is the first step towards dismantling it, transforming digital spaces into supportive environments.

### The Digital Stigma Landscape

The anonymity and distance of cyberspace can embolden some to express stigmatizing views on mental health. Misinformation spreads easily, and harmful stereotypes persist, creating an atmosphere where people might hesitate to seek help or share their experiences. This digital stigma reinforces existing biases and hinders access to support and understanding.

### Counteracting Negativity

Combating online stigma requires a multi-pronged approach. One effective strategy involves actively challenging misinformation and stereotypes when encountered. You can do this by politely engaging in discussions, providing accurate information from trusted sources, or simply offering words of support to counter negativity. Another approach is to create and share content that sheds light on mental health issues. Sharing personal stories or using scientific evidence can foster a more balanced understanding. By flooding digital spaces with positive and accurate representations of mental health, we can begin to shift the tide.

### Leveraging Influencers and Communities

Social media influencers and online communities have the power to shape online narratives and can be valuable allies in the fight against stigma. Influencers, with their large followings, can play a crucial role by sharing their own experiences, promoting healthy discussions, and raising awareness about mental health. Similarly, online communities focused on mental health provide safe spaces for people to seek advice, share stories, and find support. These communities can also organize online campaigns to challenge stigma or support those facing discrimination.

### Personal Empowerment

Empowering individuals to share their stories and advocate for themselves is vital in overcoming stigma. While daunting, sharing your experience with mental health challenges online can be incredibly powerful. It offers hope and inspiration to others struggling in silence and challenges misconceptions that fuel stigma. Encouraging self-advocacy involves providing people with the tools and platforms to share their experiences, whether through social media, blogs, or online forums dedicated to mental health.

Overcoming the complexities of mental health stigma in cyberspace requires a collective effort. By challenging negative narratives, leveraging the influence of digital communities, and empowering individuals to share their stories, we can dismantle the barriers that stigma erects. In doing so, we can transform the digital landscape into a space that supports, rather than hinders, mental health and well-being.

## 1.10 From Comparison to Compassion: Reframing Social Media Interactions

Social media is often filled with carefully curated snapshots of success, beauty, and seemingly perfect lives. This constant bombardment can lead many users down a path of unhealthy comparison, known as the "comparison trap." This trap can significantly diminish our self-worth and satisfaction with life. The curated feeds we see rarely reflect the struggles and setbacks that are part of the human experience, creating a distorted perception of reality. Recognizing this trap is the first step towards cultivating a healthier relationship with social media, one rooted in compassion rather than comparison. Here's how you can make the shift:

**Promoting Compassion**

Compassion, built on understanding and empathy, is the key to transforming social media interactions. Start by consciously consuming content that fosters these values. Follow accounts that share stories of struggles and resilience, celebrate diversity and inclusion, and promote kindness and support. Filling your feed with positive and uplifting content encourages a more compassionate viewpoint.

**Actively Contributing to Empathy**

Next, actively contribute to an environment of empathy and understanding. This could be as simple as leaving supportive comments on posts, sharing content that resonates with our shared human experiences, or sending a private message to someone letting them know you understand. These small gestures can ripple through the online community, fostering a more connected and empathetic space.

**Mindful Engagement**

Mindful engagement with social media requires us to be present and intentional with our interactions. Before scrolling through your feed, take a moment to check in with yourself. How are you feeling? What are you hoping to gain from this experience? If you're seeking connection, look for posts that interest you and engage with them thoughtfully. If you notice you're starting to spiral into comparison, permit yourself to step away.

Here are a few practices to encourage mindfulness on social media:

**Pause Before You Post:** Consider the intention behind your share. Is it to connect, to inspire, to educate? Ensuring your content aligns with your values fosters more meaningful interactions.

**Reflect on Your Reactions:** When you feel envy or inadequacy creeping in as you scroll, take a moment to reflect on why. Understanding your triggers can help you navigate your social media use more mindfully.

**Gratitude Posting:** Regularly share what you're grateful for. This shifts your focus from what you lack to what you have and encourages others to do the same.

**Building Supportive Networks**

Creating and participating in online networks that support mental health can significantly enhance your social media experience. These networks serve as safe havens where individuals can share openly without fear of judgment, seek advice, and find solidarity. Here's how to cultivate such spaces:

**Seek Out Positive Communities:** Many social media platforms host groups centered around mental health support, hobby-based communities, or groups dedicated to personal growth. Joining these can offer a sense of belonging and a reminder that you're not alone in your struggles.

**Be an Active Member:** Don't just lurk. Share your stories, ask questions, and offer support. The more you engage, the more valuable these communities become for you and others.

**Create Your Own Space:** If you can't find the right community, consider starting your own. Whether it's a private group for friends to share and support each other or a public page focused on a specific aspect of mental health, taking the initiative can be incredibly rewarding.

**Set Boundaries:** Encourage healthy interactions by establishing clear guidelines for engagement within any group or space you create or participate in. This helps maintain a supportive, respectful environment for all members.

For all its pitfalls, social media holds the potential to be a powerful tool for positive change. By shifting our focus from comparison to compassion, engaging mindfully, and fostering supportive networks, we can transform our digital interactions into sources of strength and solidarity. Imagine the possibilities: social media campaigns raising awareness for mental health, online communities offering support groups for those struggling, and a digital landscape that celebrates diversity and understanding. This approach not only benefits our mental well-being but also contributes to a broader cultural shift towards empathy in the digital age. So, why not take the first step today? Follow an inspiring account, leave a supportive comment, or share a message of kindness. Together, we can rewrite the narrative of social media, one compassionate interaction at a time.

## 1.11 Building a Supportive Online Community for Mental Health

Online communities dedicated to mental health support offer a unique platform for individuals to connect, share experiences, and find encouragement on their journeys to well-being. Unlike traditional support groups, these online spaces provide a level of anonymity and accessibility that can be particularly helpful for those hesitant to seek help in person. However, fostering a truly supportive and effective online community isn't simply a matter of creating a forum. It requires careful consideration of several key elements that ensure its effectiveness and longevity.

**Community Foundations**

What sets a supportive online mental health community apart is its ability to foster an environment of empathy, respect, and understanding. This environment is cultivated through:

**Shared Goals:** Clearly defining the purpose of the community, whether it's to support anxiety disorders, depression, or another specific focus, helps align members towards a common goal.

**Inclusivity:** An influential community welcomes members from all walks of life, acknowledging the diverse experiences and perspectives they bring. This diversity enriches the community, offering a broader range of insights and support.

**Openness and Honesty:** It is crucial to encourage members to share their true feelings, challenges, and successes in a non-judgmental space. It creates a culture of authenticity that can deeply resonate with others.

**Participation and Engagement**

Active contribution and engagement from members are the lifeblood of any online community. Here are strategies that encourage active participation:

**Encourage Story Sharing:** Prompting members to share their stories can be a powerful engagement tool. It helps individuals feel seen and heard and demonstrates to others that they are not alone in their struggles.

**Host Regular Activities:** Organizing regular events, such as live Q&A sessions with mental health professionals, themed discussion threads, or virtual meetups, keeps the community dynamic and engaged.

**Reward Participation:** Recognizing active members through badges, shoutouts, or other forms of recognition can motivate continued participation and contribution.

### Safety and Privacy

Creating a safe space for members to share and interact is paramount. This involves:

**Clear Guidelines:** Establishing and enforcing clear community guidelines helps maintain a respectful and supportive atmosphere. These guidelines should address topics like confidentiality, respectful communication, and the handling of sensitive content.

**Privacy Controls:** Educating members on using privacy settings and controls within the platform empowers them to manage their personal information and interactions according to their comfort levels.

**Moderation Team:** A dedicated team of moderators trained to handle sensitive situations, mediate conflicts, and ensure adherence to community guidelines is essential. This team is the community's safeguard, maintaining its integrity and safety.

### Sustaining Community Health

For an online mental health community to thrive, it must evolve and adapt to the needs of its members while maintaining its core health. This requires:

**Regular Feedback Loops:** Implementing mechanisms for collecting and acting on member feedback ensures that the community remains relevant and responsive to its members' needs.

**Resource Sharing:** Providing access to mental health resources, such as articles, toolkits, and crisis helplines, supports the community's educational aspect. It's about offering more than just a space for conversation but also a portal to valuable information.

**Well-being Checks:** Regularly checking in on the community's overall health, possibly through surveys or informal discussions, helps identify areas for improvement or intervention. It's a proactive approach to community management, ensuring issues are addressed before they escalate.

Building a supportive online community for mental health is a dynamic process rooted in empathy, engagement, safety, and continuous improvement. In the digital age, navigating the complexities of mental health can be particularly challenging. Social media comparison fuels anxieties, information overload can leave us feeling overwhelmed, and the very nature of online interactions can sometimes create a sense of isolation. However, well-designed online communities can act as havens of support, offering solace, guidance, and a sense of belonging to those struggling. By focusing on these foundational elements - empathy, engagement, safety, and continuous improvement - these communities can empower individuals on their journeys toward mental well-being.

# Chapter 2: The Dawn of Mindful Mornings

Imagine starting your day differently. Instead of the usual alarm jolt and mad dash, what if you began with a few quiet moments of reflection and focus? This shift, from reactive scrambling to intentional action, could have a profound impact on your entire day. This chapter explores the transformative power of a simple five-minute mindfulness routine practiced right after waking up.

In our fast-paced world, prioritizing well-being over productivity might seem like a luxury. However, a mindful morning routine is like tuning an instrument before a performance. Those few moments of self-care ensure you approach the day with clarity and calmness, creating a more harmonious experience. Here's how a simple, accessible routine can set the stage for a positive and focused day.

### 2.1 The Five-Minute Mindfulness Morning Routine

#### Efficiency of Simplicity

The beauty of this routine lies in its ease and minimal time commitment. Just like a morning coffee signals wakefulness, a brief mindfulness exercise alerts your mind to shift gears, entering the day with peace instead of panic. We're not talking about a complete morning overhaul or forcing yourself into meditation before dawn. The goal is to integrate small, manageable practices into your existing routine.

#### Routine Examples

Here's a simple five-minute routine that can significantly impact your day:

**Deep Breaths:** Before leaving bed, take some deep breaths. Inhale slowly through your nose, filling your lungs and abdomen, then exhale completely. Repeat this five times. This type of breathing activates your body's relaxation response, promoting calmness.

**Gratitude Reflection:** Take a moment to think of three things you're grateful for. These can be big things like family and health, or small things like the warmth of your blanket. Focusing on gratitude shifts your mindset from worries and tasks to appreciation, starting your day with a sense of contentment.

**Setting Intentions:** To conclude your routine, set an intention for the day. This could be a specific attitude you want to cultivate, like patience or openness, or a goal you wish to achieve. Setting intentions directs your mental energy, providing a compass for navigating your day.

### Adaptability

The key is to personalize this routine. Not a fan of lying down for deep breathing? Try standing by an open window, letting the fresh air invigorate you as you breathe. Don't connect with gratitude reflection? Perhaps a moment of visualization, picturing your ideal day unfolding, would resonate better. The routine should feel like a natural extension of your morning, not a chore.

### Long-term Benefits

The magic happens with consistency. Over time, this small investment of five minutes can significantly improve your mental well-being. You might experience reduced stress, improved focus, and a more positive outlook. Think of it like building interest on your well-being; the benefits accumulate and multiply each day, leading to lasting changes in your mental state.

This isn't just about starting your day differently; it's about reclaiming your mornings. Transform them from grogginess and stress into a moment of peace and empowerment. It's a small shift with the potential for profound changes, setting a positive tone that carries through your entire day.

## 2.2 Cognitive Behavioral Techniques for the Busy Mind

In the daily hustle, our minds can become battlegrounds for stress and negativity. But amidst this chaos, Cognitive Behavioral Therapy (CBT) emerges as a powerful tool for taking control. At its core, CBT is a therapeutic approach that helps us identify and challenge unhelpful thought patterns, emotions, and behaviors. These patterns often lead to problems like anxiety, depression, and low self-esteem. The good news is, the principles of CBT can be distilled into practical, everyday strategies, offering a lifeline for those grappling with the pressures of a busy life.

CBT works because our thoughts, feelings, and behaviors are interconnected. A negative thought can trigger feelings of anxiety, which can then lead to avoidance behaviors that reinforce the initial thought. By changing one element in this cycle, we can disrupt the entire pattern and create a more positive experience.

### Techniques on-the-go

Finding time for therapy sessions isn't always easy, but CBT's beauty lies in its adaptability. Here are some quick strategies you can employ anywhere:

**The Two-Minute Rule:** When a negative thought pops up, acknowledge it for two minutes, then shift your focus to a calming activity or a positive thought. Over time, this practice weakens the negative thoughts held in your mind.

**Breathing for Calm:** Focused breathing can act as a bridge to mindfulness. Inhale deeply for a count of four, hold for four, and exhale for four. This simple technique can center your thoughts and help you break the cycle of negativity.

**Self-talk adjustments**

Our inner voice plays a crucial role in shaping how we see the world and react to situations. CBT emphasizes identifying and modifying negative self-talk:

**Identify and Challenge:** First, recognize instances of harmful or self-critical thoughts. Challenge them by asking yourself evidence-based questions like, "What proof do I have that this thought is true?" or "Is there another way to look at this?"

**Reframing:** Once you've identified and challenged a negative thought, reframe it into a more realistic or positive one. For example, if you think, "I can't handle this," reframe it to, "This is challenging, but I can break it down and work through it step by step."

**Application in daily situations**

The beauty of CBT is that you can integrate its techniques seamlessly into your daily life. Here are some examples:

**At Work:** Feeling overwhelmed? Use the "chunking" method, breaking down large tasks into smaller, manageable steps. Pair this with reframing thoughts from "I'll never get this done" to "I'm making progress, one step at a time."

**In Relationships:** During family or social conflicts, practice "perspective-taking" by considering the situation from the other person's point of view. This can help you moderate your reaction and approach the conflict with empathy.

CBT is more than just a therapeutic approach; it's a toolkit for life. By incorporating these strategies into your daily routine, you're not just moving away from negative thoughts, you're actively steering towards a more balanced and positive mental state. If you'd like to learn more about CBT, there are many excellent self-help books and online courses available. Remember, you have the power to take control of your thoughts and build a more resilient mind.

## 2.3 Quick Grounding Techniques for Immediate Relief

In the daily grind, anxiety and stress can feel ever-present. Fortunately, there's a toolbox of techniques called grounding techniques that can quickly bring us back to a state of calm and presence. Grounding techniques, rooted in mindfulness and sensory awareness, help us shift focus away from distress and anchor ourselves firmly in the present moment. These methods offer immediate relief and can be practiced anywhere, anytime.

Grounding techniques work by diverting our attention from anxious thoughts towards the immediate environment and bodily sensations. This simple act of refocusing disrupts the cycle of stress and anxiety, promoting a sense of control and easing overwhelming emotions.

### Five Senses Method

A widely used and highly effective grounding technique involves engaging all five senses to bring awareness to the present. Here's how you can implement this method:

**See:** Look around and name five things you can see. It could be the color of the wall, a plant on the windowsill, or simply the pattern on your shoes.

**Touch:** Notice four things you can feel. This might be the texture of your clothing, the smooth surface of a table, or the weight of a book in your hand.

**Hear:** Listen for three sounds. It could be distant traffic, birds chirping outside, or the hum of a computer.

**Smell:** Identify two things you can smell. If you can't immediately smell anything, walk to a window or, if possible, outside. Or, smell your wrist where you might have perfume or a soap scent.

**Taste:** Acknowledge one thing you can taste. This could be the aftertaste of a meal or drink, or maybe you have a piece of gum or candy to help with this step.

Walking through this exercise redirects your focus from internal distress to external reality, easing anxiety and fostering a sense of control.

**Visualization Practices**

Visualization, or creating mental images, serves as another potent grounding technique. It helps by transporting your mind to a calmer, safer place, thus reducing feelings of stress or anxiety. Here's a simple visualization exercise to try:

Find a comfortable position, close your eyes, and take a few deep breaths to start relaxing.

Picture a safe, peaceful place. It could be a real place you've visited or an imagined setting that makes you feel secure and happy. Visualize this place in as much detail as possible: the sights, the sounds, the smells, even the temperature and textures.

Engage all your senses in this visualization. If you're imagining a beach, for instance, feel the sun's warmth on your skin, hear the waves crashing gently on the shore, smell the salt in the air, and taste the freshness of the breeze.

Stay in this mental space for a few minutes, allowing yourself to soak in the peace and tranquility.

Gradually bring your focus back to your current environment, carrying the calmness from your visualization.

This exercise can act as a mental reset, providing immediate relief from distress and anxiety.

**Accessibility**

One of the greatest strengths of grounding techniques is their accessibility. They require no special equipment or environment and can be practiced anywhere, whether at home, work or even amid a stressful event. This toolkit of quick grounding techniques means you have a ready set of strategies to effectively manage acute stress and anxiety, anytime and anywhere.

There isn't a one-size-fits-all approach to grounding techniques. Explore different methods and discover what works best for you. Some people find deep breathing exercises helpful, while others benefit from progressive muscle relaxation. The key is to identify techniques that effectively shift your focus and promote feelings of calm. With practice, grounding techniques can become a powerful tool for navigating the ups and downs of daily life.

## 2.4 The Role of Physical Exercise in Mental Health

Physical exercise isn't just good for our bodies; it's a powerful tool for nurturing our mental well-being. Exercise strengthens the undeniable connection between the body and mind, and the science behind its mood-boosting effects is compelling.

**Exercise and Endorphins**

Endorphins, often called the body's natural painkillers, play a key role in the link between exercise and mental health. These chemicals, released during physical activity, act like a dose of happiness, lifting our spirits and reducing pain. But their benefits extend beyond pain relief; endorphins also alleviate stress and anxiety, offering a sense of calm after the storm of daily worries. This biochemical reaction is like flipping a switch, illuminating negative thoughts with a surge of positivity and peace.

Engaging in any form of physical activity can trigger this endorphin release. Whether it's a brisk walk, a dance class, or a weightlifting session, movement signals the brain to send out these feel-good chemicals, paving the way for a brighter mental state.

### Incorporating Movement into Daily Life

Fitting exercise into a busy schedule might seem daunting, but the beauty of movement lies in its flexibility. There's a form of exercise for everyone, regardless of preference or lifestyle. Here are some practical tips to weave more physical activity into your day:

- Take the stairs instead of the elevator. This simple switch can have a significant impact over time.
- Park further away from your destination to sneak in a few extra steps.
- Stand or walk around during phone calls instead of sitting.
- Break up long periods of sitting with short walks or stretching sessions.
- Find active hobbies you enjoy, like gardening, dancing, or cycling.

### Types of Exercise for Mental Wellness

The range of exercise beneficial for mental health is broad, encompassing everything from cardio to strength training. Here are some types with particularly strong links to mental well-being:

**Aerobic Exercise:** Activities like running, swimming, or cycling improve cardiovascular health and have been shown to reduce symptoms of depression and anxiety.

**Yoga:** Combining physical postures, breathing exercises, and meditation, yoga enhances both mental and physical well-being.

**Walking:** Accessible to most, walking, especially in nature, can decrease stress and boost mood.

**Resistance Training**: Lifting weights or using resistance bands strengthens the body and improves mental health by reducing anxiety and depressive symptoms.

Each activity offers a unique pathway to improved mental well-being, allowing individuals to choose the exercise form that resonates most with them.

**Personal Stories of Transformation**

The real-world impact of exercise on mental health comes alive in the stories of those who've embraced physical activity and witnessed its transformative effects. Take Alex, for example, who found solace in running after a period of deep depression. The rhythmic sound of his feet hitting the pavement became a moving meditation, a time to process thoughts and emotions, leading to a significant improvement in his mood and outlook.

Then there's Jordan, who discovered yoga during a stressful career transition. The practice offered him physical release and a newfound sense of inner calm and resilience, equipping him with the mental clarity to navigate life's challenges.

These narratives highlight a common theme: exercise, in its various forms, can reshape our mental landscape, offering a sanctuary of calm, a source of strength, and a wellspring of joy. Through the lens of these personal journeys, the role of physical activity in mental health isn't just a concept but a lived reality, a testament to the transformative power of movement.

By integrating exercise into our lives, we do more than enhance our physical health; we open the door to a more vibrant and balanced state of mental well-being. Whether through endorphin release, incorporating movement into daily routines, exploring various forms of exercise, or finding inspiration from personal stories, the path to improved mental heaslth is clear. With each step, stretch, or stroke, we move closer to a state of mind marked by clarity and peace.\

## 2.5 Nightly Routines for Better Sleep and Mental Clarity

The dance between day and night shapes our lives in profound ways, with the serenity of the evening offering a perfect counterpoint to the day's hustle. This rhythm, ancient and ingrained, suggests that how we wind down at night can significantly affect our sleep quality, mental clarity, and overall well-being. Let's explore the sanctity of sleep hygiene, a concept that goes beyond mere habits to touch the essence of rejuvenation and restoration.

### The Importance of Sleep Hygiene

Sleep stands out as a critical yet often neglected thread in the tapestry of health. Its impact on mental health is as profound as it is broad, influencing mood, cognitive function, and resilience against stress. Sleep hygiene, a collection of practices that pave the way for restful sleep, emerges as a vital practice. It's about creating a nightly ritual that cues your body and mind for sleep, much like a lullaby does for a child. This ritual not only enhances sleep quality but also fortifies mental clarity, preparing you for the challenges and joys of the following day.

### Steps for a Peaceful Night

Crafting a bedtime routine that whispers to your senses and eases you into sleep involves a few key steps, each a stepping stone to a night of deep, restorative sleep:

Disconnect to Reconnect: An hour before bed, gently disengage from digital devices. The screens that dominate our day emit blue light, which can hinder the production of melatonin, the hormone that regulates sleep. Instead, this time could be spent in quieter pursuits such as reading, gentle stretching, or calming music.

Sip Towards Sleep: Consider a warm, non-caffeinated beverage like herbal tea. Chamomile, for instance, is known for its calming properties and can be a soothing prelude to sleep.

Reflect and Release: Keeping a journal by your bed invites you to pour the day's thoughts, worries, and gratitudes onto paper. This act of reflection and release can lighten your mental load, making it easier to slip into sleep.

Cultivate Comfort: Your sleeping environment plays a crucial role in the quality of your rest. Ensure your bedroom is a sanctuary designed for sleep. This means comfortable bedding, a cool temperature, and perhaps a drop of lavender oil on your pillow for its relaxing aroma.

**Environment Optimization**

A sleep-friendly environment acts as the stage for a night of restful sleep. Here are some tips to fine-tune your bedroom for optimal sleep:

Embrace the Dark: Darkness signals your brain that it's time to rest. Blackout curtains or a sleep mask can block light, reinforcing your body's natural sleep-wake cycle.

Stay Cool: The ideal temperature for sleep is around 65 degrees Fahrenheit (18 degrees Celsius). A cooler room helps lower your body temperature, a necessary step for falling asleep.

Invest in Comfort: Your mattress, pillows, and bedding should support a comfortable sleep posture. It's worth investing in high-quality sleep aids that align with your preferences and physical needs.

Hush the Noise: Consider a white noise machine or earplugs if you are easily disturbed by outside noises. The consistent sound of white noise can mask abrupt changes in the environment, helping maintain a serene atmosphere.

### Dealing with Sleep Disruptions

Even with the best preparations, sleep disruptions can occur. Should you find yourself awake in the night, here are some strategies to coax your mind back into sleep:

Stay Calm: Avoid watching the clock, as this can increase stress. Remember that rest is still beneficial, even if you're not asleep.

Mindful Breathing: Deep breaths can help soothe your nervous system into a state of relaxation. Focus on the rhythm of your breathing to draw your mind away from wakeful thoughts.

Change of Scene: If sleep eludes you for more than 20 minutes, consider getting up and engaging in a low-stimulus activity in another room, such as reading or knitting, until you feel sleepy again.

Limit Daytime Naps: To ensure you're sufficiently tired at bedtime, keep daytime naps short (20-30 minutes) and avoid napping late in the day.

By weaving these practices into the fabric of your evenings, you're not just preparing for a night of sleep but setting the stage for days marked by greater mental clarity, emotional balance, and vibrant health. Sleep hygiene, with its rituals and routines, becomes an act of self-care, a nightly renewal that supports your journey through the waking hours with grace and resilience.

## 2.6 Designing Your Mental Health Plan

Taking charge of your mental health is like charting a course for uncharted territory. It requires a personalized plan, a roadmap that guides you from your current state to your desired state of well-being. This isn't about setting unrealistic goals that are impossible to achieve. Instead, it's about establishing actionable steps that will lead to genuine improvements in your mental health.

**Blueprint for Wellness**

The first step is to assess your current mental health landscape. What aspects of your life feel balanced and fulfilling? Are there areas that cause you stress or dissatisfaction? This initial assessment doesn't need to be overly detailed, but it should provide a clear starting point for your plan.

Next, envision what an improved state of mental health would look like for you. This vision serves as the foundation of your roadmap, guiding the specific goals and strategies you'll establish.

**Setting Realistic Goals**

Realistic and achievable goals are the cornerstones of any effective mental health plan. They act as guideposts, directing your journey towards a healthier state of mind. To set SMART goals, consider using the following framework:

**Specific:** Clearly define what you want to achieve.

**Measurable:** Establish a way to track your progress.

**Attainable:** Set goals that are challenging yet achievable.

**Relevant:** Ensure your goals align with your overall vision for mental well-being.

**Time-bound:** Set a timeframe for achieving each goal.

For example, instead of a vague goal like "feel less stressed," aim for something more concrete: "Practice 10 minutes of mindfulness meditation five days a week for one month." This approach clarifies what success looks like and makes it easier to track your progress.

### Incorporating Daily Practices

Integrating mental health practices into your daily routine is essential for bringing your plan to life. Consider small, achievable steps you can take each day to move closer to your goals. This might involve dedicating morning time to journaling, setting aside moments for deep breathing exercises to manage stress, or establishing a nightly routine that promotes restful sleep. The key is consistency; even the most minor practices, when done regularly, can yield significant benefits over time.

### Review and Adapt

Your mental health plan is a living document, meant to evolve as you do. Schedule regular reviews to ensure it aligns with your needs and goals. Reflect on what's working, what isn't, and what might need to change. This could involve setting new goals, tweaking your daily practices, or even redefining what mental wellness means to you.

Throughout this process, be kind to yourself. Progress in mental health is rarely linear, and there may be setbacks along the way. Don't view these as failures; instead, see them as opportunities for learning and growth. Ask yourself what obstacles you encountered and how you might overcome them. Perhaps a goal was too ambitious, and a smaller, more manageable target is needed. Or maybe unforeseen challenges arose, necessitating a shift in strategy. Whatever the case, these reviews are a chance to recalibrate and recommit to your journey towards better mental health.

Your mental health plan is more than a checklist of goals and activities; it's a commitment to your well-being. It acknowledges that mental health, just like physical health, requires ongoing attention, care, and maintenance. By setting realistic goals, incorporating daily practices, and regularly reviewing and adapting your plan, you're taking proactive steps towards a more balanced and fulfilling life. Remember, this plan is for you, crafted by you, and its success lies in its ability to reflect and support your unique path toward mental wellness.

## 2.7 The Power of Micro-Meditations Throughout Your Day

In our fast-paced world, it's easy to miss the quiet moments that offer a refuge from the daily grind. However, there's a simple practice that can transform fleeting moments into opportunities for peace: micro-meditations.

These brief, focused meditation sessions – lasting only a few minutes – are designed to seamlessly fit into the cracks of even the busiest schedules. Their beauty lies in their simplicity and the profound impact they can have on our overall well-being when practiced consistently.

### Defining Micro-Meditations

Micro-meditations focus on harnessing the core elements of meditation – awareness, breath, and present-moment focus – in short bursts. Unlike longer meditation practices that require dedicated time and space, micro-meditations are about integrating mindfulness into the moments we already have.

They can be as simple as taking a single mindful breath or a minute of focused attention. The goal isn't to escape from our day but to weave mindfulness into its fabric, transforming ordinary moments into mini-sanctuaries of calm.

### Finding Opportunities for Mindfulness

Our days are filled with opportunities for micro-meditation, waiting to be discovered. Here are a few examples:

**Standing in line:** Instead of reaching for your phone, use this time to center yourself with a few deep breaths.

**During your commute:** If you're not driving, close your eyes for a moment and focus on the sensation of movement. If you're walking, pay attention to the feeling of each step.

**Before a new task:** Take a minute to clear your mind and set an intention for the task at hand.

Savor your coffee or tea: Pay full attention to the taste, temperature, and aroma of each sip.

These snippets of time, often lost to daydreams or the digital world, hold the potential for significant mental refreshment when approached with mindfulness.

**Simple Techniques to Start**

Micro-meditations are accessible to everyone – no fancy equipment or lengthy prep work required. Here are a few techniques you can try right away:

**One-Minute Breath Focus:** Close your eyes and simply focus on your breath for a minute. Breathe deeply and slowly, noticing the physical sensations of inhaling and exhaling.

**Sensory Awareness:** Choose one sense to focus on for a few moments. Perhaps listen intently to the sounds around you, or pick up an object and concentrate on its texture.

**Gratitude Burst:** Take a moment to appreciate something in your life, no matter how small. Let the feeling of gratitude wash over you.

These practices are more than just a quick mental break; they're building blocks for a more mindful way of living. They help you cultivate a sense of presence and peace throughout your day.

### Cumulative Impact

The true benefit of micro-meditations unfolds over time. At first, the effects might seem subtle – a fleeting improvement in mood or a brief moment of clarity. But as you integrate these practices into your daily routine, their cumulative impact becomes undeniable. You might find yourself reacting more calmly to stress or feeling more connected to the present moment. Over time, micro-meditations can lead to a significant shift in how you experience your inner and outer world, boosting your mental well-being and promoting a sense of peace even amidst life's challenges.

By embracing micro-meditations, we tap into the transformative power of mindfulness, one moment at a time. This approach doesn't require carving out extra hours from your day; it's about bringing a different level of awareness to the time you already have. It's an invitation to sprinkle your daily life with moments of presence, focus, and tranquility, transforming the ordinary into a gateway to something extraordinary. Micro-meditation helps us discover that peace isn't a faraway destination, but a path we walk step-by-mindful-step, each and every day.

## 2.8 Leveraging Technology for Mindfulness Practices

Our smartphones often get a bad rap for contributing to stress. But there's a flip side: with the right approach, these devices can become powerful allies in our quest for calm and focus. It's all about using technology intentionally to harness the power of mindfulness and meditation.

### Tech as a Tool

The key is understanding that technology itself is neutral. It's how we use it that matters. Smartphones are packed with mindfulness apps and features – from guided meditations that fit your coffee break to calming sounds that drown out the noise of your commute. These tools are at your fingertips, waiting to be used.

The trick is to shift your perspective. See your phone not as a distraction, but as a gateway to mindfulness. There are tons of resources available, so the challenge is finding ones that fit your needs and lifestyle.

**App Recommendations**

To get you started, here are a few highly-rated mindfulness apps:

**Insight Timer:** This app offers a huge library of free guided meditations on various topics, from stress relief to sleep. It even has a community feature that connects you with other meditators around the world.

**Ten Percent Happier:** Ideal for beginners and skeptics, this app takes the mystery out of meditation with practical, approachable sessions led by well-known teachers. It focuses on the real-world benefits of meditation, making it a great tool for integrating mindfulness into daily life.

**Calm:** Known for its beautiful design and soothing soundscapes, Calm offers guided sessions for reducing anxiety, improving sleep, and boosting focus. Their bedtime stories for adults have become a popular choice for promoting restful sleep.

**Breathe2Relax:** This app focuses specifically on the stress-reducing power of breathing exercises. It guides users through diaphragmatic breathing techniques, offering a quick and easy way to center yourself during moments of anxiety.

These are just a few options, and each app has its own unique features and approach. Experiment with a few to find what works best for you on your mindfulness journey.

### Setting Reminders

Your phone can also help you seamlessly weave mindfulness practices into your daily routine. Setting reminders is a simple yet effective way to do this. Whether it's a prompt for a midday breathing exercise or a reminder to unwind with a guided meditation before bed, these digital cues can gently nudge you to pause and connect with the present moment.

Setting reminders is as easy as using your phone's built-in alarm or calendar app. The key is to schedule them at times you're likely to follow through, so they become regular touchstones of calm in your day.

### Balancing Digital with Real-Life

While technology offers valuable support for mindfulness, it's important to maintain a balance between digital and real-life experiences. Mindfulness is all about connecting with the present moment, something that's enriched by directly engaging with the world around us.

Here are some tips to ensure technology enhances, rather than hinders, your mindfulness efforts:

**Be Mindful of What You Consume:** Be selective about the apps and content you use. Choose resources that contribute to your well-being, and avoid those that are distracting or upsetting.

**Schedule Tech-Free Time:** Dedicate specific times of day to be tech-free. This could be during meals, your first hour after waking, or before bed. These digital pauses can amplify your mindfulness practice and encourage you to directly experience the world around you.

**Tech for Nature:** Use technology to enhance real-life mindfulness experiences. There are apps that can identify plants, birds, or stars, turning a simple walk in the park into an immersive mindfulness session.

**Digital Detox Regularly:** Schedule regular digital detoxes to reset your relationship with technology. This gives you space to reflect on how to best integrate digital tools into your mindfulness practice.

By using technology thoughtfully, we can harness its potential to expand and enrich our mindfulness journey. It's about finding harmony, ensuring our digital interactions support our quest for mental clarity and inner peace. With the right approach, our devices can transform from sources of distraction to gateways of mindfulness, offering a touch of serenity right in the palm of our hands.

## 2.9 Saying No: Establishing Boundaries for Mental Health

Imagine a personal fortress that safeguards your well-being. That's what healthy boundaries are – a way to protect your mental health by recognizing your worth, understanding your limits, and making choices that prioritize your well-being. This guide explores the foundational steps for setting boundaries that empower you and strengthen your relationships.

### Boundary Basics

Boundaries are all about self-respect and self-care. They're about defining what's acceptable in your interactions with others. This clarity allows you to navigate relationships more effectively, ensuring your needs are met. The first step is understanding yourself. Ask yourself:

- What are my limits?
- What values are important to me?
- What aspects of my life are non-negotiable?
- What do I need to feel respected, supported, and content?

### Assertiveness Training

Successfully setting and maintaining boundaries requires assertiveness. This means finding the sweet spot between being a pushover and overly aggressive. It's about clearly and respectfully expressing your needs and desires without disrespecting others. Here are some tips to hone your assertiveness:

**Speak Your Truth:** Use "I" statements to express your feelings and needs without blaming others. For instance, "I feel overwhelmed when I take on extra tasks. I need to focus on my current workload."

**Practice Makes Perfect:** Role-play how you'd assert yourself in different situations with a trusted friend or in front of a mirror. This builds confidence and helps you find the right words on the spot.

**Begin Small:** Start by putting yourself in low-pressure scenarios. This could be something simple like choosing the restaurant for a get-together.

### Real-life Scenarios

Setting boundaries in both personal and professional settings can significantly improve your mental health. Here are some examples to guide you:

**With Friends:** If a friend frequently cancels plans last minute, you could say, "I understand things happen, but it's frustrating when plans are canceled at the last minute. Moving forward, can we try to be more reliable with scheduling?"

**At Work:** When faced with more work than you can handle, consider responding with, "I recognize this project is important, but I'm already stretched thin. Can we discuss prioritizing tasks or delegating some of the workload?"

**Respecting Your Limits**

A crucial aspect of boundaries is honoring your limits. This means recognizing when you're overloaded and taking steps to protect your energy and well-being. Here's how to get started:

**Regular Check-Ins:** Make it a habit to assess your energy levels and feelings throughout the day. Are you feeling drained or overwhelmed? What's causing these feelings?

**Identify Your Red Flags:** Pay attention to signs that a boundary may be needed. This could include feeling resentful, uncomfortable, or stressed in certain situations or relationships.

**Self-Care is Not Selfish:** Remember that saying no to others sometimes allows you to say yes to yourself. Prioritizing your well-being isn't selfish; it's essential.

Setting boundaries is a continuous process that adapts to your needs and circumstances. Be patient, practice regularly, and be kind to yourself. By embracing your right to establish limits, you safeguard your mental health and cultivate more fulfilling and honest relationships. Remember, when you prioritize your needs, you allow others to understand and respect them as well.

## 2.10 Practical Self-Care for the Overwhelmed Soul

In the hustle and bustle of everyday life, self-care often gets pushed aside. We might see it as a treat, something extra we don't have time for. But that's a mistake. Self-care isn't a luxury; it's as essential to our well-being as food and water are to our physical health.

**Self-Care Redefined**

Think of self-care as the foundation for a healthy relationship with yourself. It's the deliberate act of taking care of our mental, emotional, and physical needs. By prioritizing our well-being, we become better equipped to handle life's challenges and show up for the people in our lives. Just like we can't pour from an empty cup, taking care of ourselves allows us to give more to others.

### Simple Self-Care Actions

The beauty of self-care is that it doesn't have to be complicated or expensive. Here are some easy but effective ways to boost your mental well-being:

**Nature Walks:** Spending time outdoors can do wonders for your mind. A walk in the park can clear your head and reduce stress.

**Digital Detox:** Schedule unplugged time each day to disconnect from your devices. This break from information overload allows for some much-needed reflection.

**Mindful Meals:** Turn mealtimes into self-care moments by eating mindfully. Slow down, savor each bite, and appreciate the nourishment you're giving your body.

**Creative Expression:** Engage in activities that spark your creativity, like drawing, writing, or playing music. Creativity is a great emotional outlet and can leave you feeling accomplished and happy.

**Self-Compassion Breaks:** Throughout your day, take a moment for self-compassion. Talk to yourself with kindness, acknowledge your efforts, and forgive yourself for any mistakes.

### Incorporating Self-Care into Routines

The key to making self-care a regular part of your life is to weave it into your daily routine. Here are some tips:

**Morning Intentions:** Start your day by setting a positive intention for yourself. This could be a simple affirmation or a reminder to be kind to yourself.

**Scheduled Self-Care Breaks:** Plan short breaks throughout your day specifically for self-care. A 10-minute break to stretch, meditate, or take some deep breaths can make a big difference in your energy levels.

**Evening Wind-Down Routine:** Create a relaxing evening routine to signal to your body that it's time to unwind. This could include reading, taking a warm bath, or doing some gentle yoga.

**Gratitude Journal:** Before bed, jot down a few things you're grateful for. Focusing on gratitude helps cultivate a positive mindset and can even improve your sleep quality.

**Overcoming Self-Care Guilt**

A common hurdle to self-care is feeling guilty about taking time for ourselves, especially in cultures that glorify busyness and self-sacrifice. It's important to overcome this guilt and see self-care as a non-negotiable part of maintaining your mental health. Here's how to combat self-care guilt:

**Shift Your Perspective:** Reframe self-care as a way to recharge. By taking care of yourself, you'll be more present and effective in all your roles. It's not selfish, it's strategic.

**Communicate Your Needs:** Talk to your friends and family about your self-care practices. Sharing your experience can normalize self-care and encourage others to prioritize their well-being too.

**Start Small:** If you struggle with guilt, begin with small acts of self-care. As you experience the benefits, you'll become more comfortable dedicating more time to your well-being.

**Seek Support:** If guilt remains a significant barrier, consider talking to a therapist or counselor. They can help you manage these feelings and develop a healthier approach to self-care.

Self-care is all about changing our mindset. By viewing it as essential maintenance for our mental health, we can significantly improve our well-being. Incorporating simple self-care practices into our routines and overcoming self-care guilt are crucial steps in this journey. Through consistent effort, self-care becomes a way of life, honoring our needs and nurturing our inner selves. This allows us to face life's challenges with resilience and grace.

## 2.11 The Importance of Mental Health Days in the Workplace

In today's fast-paced work environment, where productivity often reigns supreme, mental health days are emerging as a powerful tool for maintaining balance and self-awareness. Recognizing when to hit the pause button and step back isn't just about self-care; it's a strategic move that boosts long-term productivity and well-being. It's the first step towards a healthier relationship with work and yourself.

### Recognizing the Need

Understanding when a mental health day is necessary involves listening to your mental and emotional cues. Here are some signs to watch for:

**Constant stress or anxiety:** Even after relaxation techniques, these feelings linger.

**Productivity slump:** You notice a significant decrease in how much you get done, your creativity stalls, or motivation takes a nosedive.

**Trouble focusing:** Tasks that were once manageable now feel overwhelming, and concentration becomes difficult.

**Emotional red flags:** You're feeling irritable, sad, or disconnected from your work and colleagues.

Being honest with yourself about these signs and acknowledging the need for a break is crucial. It's a proactive approach to preventing burnout, not a reactive one after you're already fried.

**Negotiating Mental Health Days**

Bringing up mental health days with your boss might seem intimidating. However, with a clear and honest approach that emphasizes mutual benefit, you can have a productive conversation:

**Timing is key:** Pick a time to talk when neither of you are under pressure.

**Be upfront:** Clearly state your need for a day off, highlighting how a mental health break will positively impact your work quality and productivity.

Reassurance goes a long way: Reiterate your commitment to your role and discuss how your responsibilities will be handled while you're out, whether through delegation or adjusted deadlines.

**Maximizing the Benefit**

To ensure your mental health day truly restores you, a plan with a focus on rejuvenation is key:

**Disconnect completely:** Cut off work communication to give your mind a true break from job-related stressors.

**Do what recharges you:** Whether it's spending time in nature, a therapy session, or simply catching up on sleep, choose activities that genuinely bring you back to life.

**Skip the chores:** Resist the urge to tackle errands or personal projects. The goal is to lighten your mental load, not swap it for something else.

## Changing Workplace Culture

The conversation around mental health days is part of a larger movement to create a workplace culture that prioritizes mental well-being. Encouraging mental health days benefits not just individual employees but also the organization as a whole:

**A happier, healthier workforce:** When employees feel supported, satisfaction and retention go up.

**Destigmatizing mental health:** Open discussions make it easier for everyone to talk about mental health and seek help when needed.

**A more balanced approach:** It acknowledges that rest and recovery are just as important to productivity as hard work and dedication.

By integrating mental health days into company policies, businesses show their commitment to employee well-being. This approach fosters a more compassionate, productive, and sustainable work environment where individual health thrives.

As we navigate the complexities of work and mental health, mental health days represent a shift in how we understand productivity and well-being. They challenge the notion that constant work equals success, instead offering a vision of balance where rest is recognized as a crucial component of achievement. This shift empowers individuals and shapes a workplace culture that values the human behind the employee, creating a space where well-being and work can coexist in harmony.

Integrating mental health days into the workplace signifies a significant step toward a more balanced and healthy approach to work and well-being. It highlights the importance of recognizing our limits, advocating for our needs, and taking deliberate steps to safeguard our mental health. As we move forward, this conversation opens the door for deeper discussions on mental well-being in the professional sphere, inviting us to redefine what a healthy work-life balance truly looks like.

# Chapter 3: Crafting Your Path to Wellness

Imagine a closet overflowing with clothes, yet nothing seems to fit quite right. That's how mental health solutions can feel sometimes: one-size-fits-all approaches that leave you wanting. Just like a tailor adjusts clothes to your unique body, a personalized path to mental well-being ensures the strategies you choose work for you. This guide is your fitting room, where you'll learn to assess your needs, tailor strategies, and create a personalized mental health plan that fits you perfectly.

## 3.1 Identifying Your Mental Health Needs: A Self-Assessment Guide

**Self-awareness is the first step.**

Self-awareness is key. Picture navigating a city without a map. You might eventually get where you're going, but it takes longer and is far more frustrating. The same goes for mental health – understanding your starting point is crucial. Reflect on times you felt overwhelmed or stressed. What situations triggered these feelings? Recognizing these patterns is the first step to mapping your mental health landscape.

**Comprehensive assessment tools**

Think of self-assessment tools as your mental health toolbox. These range from simple checklists to in-depth questionnaires created by mental health professionals. For example, the DASS-21 (Depression, Anxiety, and Stress Scales) or the WHO-5 Well-Being Index can give you valuable insights into your current state of mind. Many of these tools are readily available online for free.

Engaging with these assessments is like taking your mental health's measurements. There's no pass or fail; they're simply guides to help you navigate your path forward.

**Interpreting results**

Understanding your results is like reading a personalized map of your mental landscape. These assessments might reveal areas of stress or anxiety you weren't fully aware of, or confirm feelings you've been experiencing. They give you a clearer picture of what you're working with.

Here's a tip: keep a journal of your assessment results and reflections. Are there patterns? Do certain situations consistently lead to stress or anxiety? These insights highlight areas that might need more attention or different strategies.

**Actionable insights**

With your "measurements" in hand, it's time to tailor your mental health strategies. Let's say your assessments highlight high stress levels. The next step might be incorporating stress-reduction techniques into your daily routine. This could involve meditation, adjusting your schedule to reduce overwhelm, or finding activities that bring you joy and relaxation.

Remember, small, consistent changes often lead to the most impactful results. Try one new strategy at a time and observe how it affects your well-being. Keep what works and adjust what doesn't. This process is all about finding the perfect fit for you.

With these tools and insights, you can begin crafting your personalized approach to mental health. Remember, this is an ongoing journey. Just as our bodies and lives change, so too will our mental health needs. Regularly checking in with yourself, revisiting these assessment tools, and adjusting your strategies will ensure your approach remains a perfect fit, no matter where life takes you.

## 3.2 Tailoring Mindfulness Practices to Fit Your Life

Imagine your daily routine as a wardrobe. Some days call for the comfort of your favorite jeans and a cozy sweater, while others require the focus and polish of a sharp suit. Mindfulness should be like that too – adaptable and personalized to fit the unique contours of your life, reflecting your current needs and long-term goals.

### Personalizing mindfulness

The word "mindfulness" might conjure up images of silent meditation retreats or hours spent sitting perfectly still. But the core of mindfulness – being fully present and engaged in the moment – can be practiced in countless ways to suit your preferences and lifestyle. Dislike sitting still? You can find mindfulness in movement through activities like walking or yoga. The key is to simply anchor your attention in the present moment, whether it's feeling the warmth of the sun on your skin or focusing on the rhythm of your breath during exercise.

### Varied techniques

Think of mindfulness techniques like a diverse buffet. Each practice offers unique benefits and experiences, inviting you to discover what works best for you. Here are a few examples:

**Mindful Breathing**: This can be as simple as taking a few minutes to focus on your breath, anywhere and anytime.

**Body Scan Meditation:** Pay attention to each part of your body in turn, noticing any sensations or tension. This can be particularly grounding and is a great way to reconnect with your physical self.

**Walking Meditation:** Combine mindfulness with gentle exercise by focusing on the feeling of movement and the sights and sounds around you.

**Gratitude Practices:** Take time to reflect on and appreciate the positive aspects of your life. This can shift your mindset and cultivate a sense of gratitude.

Experiment with these and other techniques, noting which ones bring you the most peace and clarity. Remember, mindfulness isn't about achieving perfection; it's about enhancing your awareness and connection to the present moment.

**Integrating mindfulness into daily routines**

Incorporating mindfulness into your day doesn't require drastic changes or huge chunks of free time. It's about identifying existing moments in your routine where mindfulness can naturally fit. Here are some ideas:

**Morning Mindfulness:** Start your day with a positive intention or a few minutes of mindful breathing before getting out of bed.

**Mindful Meals:** Turn mealtimes into mindfulness exercises by slowing down, savoring each bite, and paying attention to the flavors, textures, and sensations of what you're eating.

**Mindful Breaks:** Use short breaks throughout your day to step away from your desk, stretch, or do a brief walking meditation.

**Evening Wind-Down:** End your day with a gratitude practice or a body scan meditation to help you relax and prepare for sleep.

By weaving these mindfulness practices into the fabric of your daily routine, you transform ordinary moments into opportunities for presence and peace.

**Tracking progress**

Keeping a mindfulness journal can be a powerful tool to track your progress, reflect on your experiences, and adjust your practices as needed. Consider journaling about:

**Your daily practices:** Note what you did, for how long, and which techniques you used.

**Your observations:** After each mindfulness session, write down any thoughts, feelings, or sensations you noticed. Did certain practices make you feel calmer, more focused, or more grounded?

**Adjustments and insights**: Use your journal to reflect on what's working and what isn't. Did you find that morning mindfulness sets a positive tone for your day, or that short mindfulness breaks help you maintain focus throughout the afternoon?

This journal becomes a living document of your mindfulness journey, providing valuable insights that can help you further refine and personalize your practice.

Flexibility and personalization are key to crafting your path to well-being through mindfulness. Just as you might adjust your clothing based on the weather or your mood, you can adapt your mindfulness practices to fit the ever-changing needs of your life. By exploring various techniques, integrating mindfulness into your daily routines, and tracking your progress, you can create a personalized practice that supports your mental health and enhances your overall well-being, perfectly tailored to you.

## 3.3 Cognitive Behavioral Therapy: Customizing Your Approach

Cognitive Behavioral Therapy (CBT) stands out in the mental health world for its practical, hands-on approach. It's based on the idea that our thoughts, feelings, and actions are all interconnected. By changing negative thinking patterns, we can change how we feel and behave.

For many, CBT offers a structured way to tackle challenges like depression, anxiety, stress, and phobias.

**Basics of CBT**

At its core, CBT involves identifying and challenging unhelpful thinking patterns and replacing them with more realistic and positive ones. Think of it like cleaning out a garden. You remove the weeds (negative thoughts) to make room for healthier plants (positive thoughts) to flourish.

Imagine you have a big presentation at work. CBT would involve recognizing any negative thoughts you have about it ("I'm going to mess up"). Then, you'd examine the evidence for and against this thought. Finally, you'd reframe it in a more balanced way ("I've prepared well and can handle this").

**Adapting CBT to personal needs**

CBT isn't a one-size-fits-all solution. It's more like a suit that can be adjusted to fit your individual needs and preferences. Here's how to make it work for you:

**Identify your targets:** Start by pinpointing the specific issues you want to address with CBT. Is it social anxiety, work stress, or something else entirely?

**Set achievable goals:** Define what success looks like for you. Do you want to have fewer negative thoughts, feel more relaxed in social settings, or manage stress more effectively?

**Pick your tools:** CBT offers a toolbox of strategies. Some people find cognitive restructuring (challenging negative thoughts) most helpful, while others benefit more from behavioral experiments (testing beliefs through new behaviors).

**Self-administered CBT techniques**

There are several CBT strategies you can try on your own to start making positive changes:

**Thought records:** Keep a journal of negative thoughts throughout the day. Then, challenge these thoughts by questioning their accuracy. This helps you develop a more balanced perspective.

**Behavioral activation:** To combat low mood or depression, schedule activities you enjoy or that give you a sense of accomplishment. This could be as simple as taking a walk in nature or setting aside time for a hobby.

**Mindfulness:** While mindfulness is often associated with meditation, in CBT it's about being present and fully engaged in the moment without judgment. This can help reduce overthinking and worry.

**Seeking professional guidance**

While self-directed CBT techniques can be very beneficial, working with a trained therapist can take your mental health to the next level. Here's how to find and work with a CBT therapist:

**Do your research:** Look for a therapist who specializes in CBT and has experience with your specific issues. Many therapists list their areas of expertise and treatment approaches online.

**First session expectations:** During your initial meetings, you'll discuss your goals and learn more about CBT. It's also a time to see if you feel comfortable working with the therapist.

**Homework is key:** CBT often involves "homework" or activities to practice outside of therapy sessions. This might include thought records, behavioral experiments, or practicing new skills.

**Open communication:** Be honest with your therapist about what's working and what isn't. Therapy is a collaborative process, and your feedback is essential for tailoring the approach to your needs.

By understanding CBT, you can take charge of your mental health. You can experiment with self-help techniques or seek professional guidance to deepen your practice. The goal of CBT is to empower you to manage your mental health effectively, whether you work with a therapist or on your own. CBT offers a structured yet flexible framework for understanding and improving your overall well-being.

## 3.4 Personal Stories of Unique Paths to Mental Wellness

Mental health is a personal journey, as unique as a fingerprint. It's a story woven with challenges, triumphs, and everything in between. This section explores the experiences of individuals who navigated the complexities of mental well-being, each finding their own path to success. We can draw inspiration and practical wisdom from their narratives to guide our own journeys.

### Diverse Experiences

**Alex and Art Therapy:** For some, expressing emotions can be difficult. Alex found comfort and a way to express themself through art therapy. Colors and shapes became a powerful language, leading to breakthroughs in managing anxiety.

**Jordan and Nature's Embrace:** The crowded gym and city noise intensified Jordan's stress and disconnection. A shift occurred when hiking and spending time outdoors became a regular practice. Nature's tranquility brought a sense of peace and groundedness.

**Sam and the Power of Laughter:** Laughter truly can be the best medicine. Skeptical at first, Sam discovered laughter yoga sessions as a surprising source of joy and stress relief. It highlights how unexpected paths can sometimes lead to well-being.

**Riley's Digital Detox:** In our screen-dominated world, Riley took a bold step back. A week-long digital detox, free from social media and emails, revealed a newfound clarity and deeper connection with themself and others. It sparked a commitment to regular digital breaks.

**Lessons Learned**

These stories offer valuable insights for our own approaches to mental health:

**Expression Beyond Words:** Like Alex, finding ways to express ourselves beyond words, through art, music, or dance, can unlock emotions and promote healing.

**Nature's Healing Touch:** Jordan's story reminds us of the therapeutic effects of connecting with nature. When feeling overwhelmed, seeking solace outdoors can be incredibly beneficial.

**Joy in the Unexpected:** Sam's experience with laughter yoga illustrates that embracing unconventional methods and stepping outside our comfort zone can open doors to well-being.

**The Importance of Disconnecting:** Riley's digital detox highlights the crucial role of taking breaks from technology to nurture mental health. Sometimes, turning off can be the best way to tune in.

**Motivational Impact**

These narratives serve as a beacon, illuminating the diverse paths to mental wellness. They emphasize that there's no single "right" way to achieve it. They encourage us to explore, experiment, and most importantly, listen to what resonates with our unique needs and circumstances. The journey to mental well-being is deeply personal, whether it involves creativity, nature, laughter, or quiet reflection. These stories inspire us to embrace our individuality as we travel that path.

### Community and Support

A common thread in each story is the importance of community and support. Whether it was a group of fellow hikers, an art therapy class, laughter yoga participants, or supportive friends and family who accepted the need for a digital detox, each individual found strength and encouragement through connection with others. This highlights an essential truth: although our journeys are personal, we don't have to walk them alone. Building a support network can be a game-changer for mental health. Here are some ways to cultivate that support:

**Join Interest Groups:** Connect with others who share your interests by joining a hiking club, art class, or wellness group. This can offer companionship and motivation.

**Engage in Community Events:** Participating in community events related to mental health or hobbies can broaden your support network and introduce you to new resources and practices.

**Explore Online Platforms:** If you prefer digital interaction or have limited access to in-person groups, online forums and social media groups focused on mental wellness can offer a space to share experiences, advice, and encouragement.

**Create Your Own Group:** If existing groups don't meet your needs, consider starting your own. This could be a casual meet-up for mindfulness walks, a book club focused on mental health, or a virtual support group.

These stories and the lessons they offer invite us to explore our own paths to mental wellness. Whether you find solace in creativity, nature, laughter, or community, the key is to find what works for you and actively engage with it. As we draw inspiration from the journeys of others, we're reminded that mental health is not just about reaching a destination, but also about discovering ourselves along the way.

## 3.5 The Role of Creativity in Personalized Mental Health Care

Self-care and mental health management often overlook a powerful tool: creativity. This section explores how tapping into our natural creativity can be therapeutic, offering comfort and a sense of accomplishment.

### Creativity as therapy

Creativity goes beyond just making art. It's a dynamic process where your mind has a conversation with itself. This can reveal hidden thoughts and feelings, offering a form of expression that bypasses the limitations of words. Engaging in creative activities can be a powerful way to manage emotions, reduce stress, and improve overall well-being. Whether you paint, write, craft, or play music, these activities can shift your focus away from stress and channel your energy into something meaningful and beautiful.

### Finding your creative outlet

Discovering your ideal form of creative expression involves exploration and experimentation. Here are some steps to find your creative voice:

**Think Back to What Brought You Joy:** Consider your childhood or past experiences where you felt happy while doing something specific. Did you enjoy doodling in notebooks, building elaborate block structures, or anything else?

**Experiment Without Fear:** Allow yourself to try different activities without worrying about becoming an expert. Take a pottery class, write a poem, or pick up a guitar. The goal is to explore freely without judgment.

**Pay Attention to What Clicks:** Notice which activities you find yourself looking forward to and which leave you feeling fulfilled. These are likely your creative outlets.

**Practical, creative exercises**

Here are some easy exercises to integrate creativity into your mental health routine:

**Daily Doodles:** Set aside a few minutes each day to doodle whatever comes to mind. This can be a relaxing way to visually express your emotions and thoughts.

**Creative Writing Prompts:** Use prompts to spark your imagination and write for ten minutes without stopping. Don't worry about writing something perfect or coherent. This exercise is about letting your thoughts flow freely.

**Nature Crafts:** Collect natural materials like leaves, stones, or flowers to create art. This activity combines the therapeutic effects of nature with creative expression.

**Photography Walks:** Go for a walk and take pictures of anything that catches your eye. This encourages mindfulness and helps you see your surroundings in a new light.

**Documenting the journey**

Keeping track of your creative journey can enhance the therapeutic benefits. Here are some ways to document your progress:

**Creative Journals:** Dedicate a journal to your creative pursuits. Paste in your doodles, write reflections on your writing, or attach photos of your crafts. Over time, this journal will become a collection of your work and a visual representation of your mental health journey.

**Blogging:** Starting a blog to share your creations can provide a sense of community and feedback. It's a platform to share your journey, insights, and connect with others who share your interests.

**Progress Photos**: If your creative outlet involves something more physical, like pottery or sculpture, take pictures at different stages of your projects. This visual timeline can be a powerful reminder of your growth and development.

Creativity offers a unique path to managing mental health. It provides a space for expression, exploration, and healing. By finding your creative outlet, engaging in accessible exercises, and documenting your journey, you open doors to personal growth and well-being. Remember, in mental health care, creativity isn't about creating masterpieces; it's about the journey of exploration, expression, and self-discovery.

## 3.6 Understanding and Utilizing Neuroplasticity for Personal Growth

For a long time, scientists believed the brain was pretty much set after a certain age. But now we know it's more like a dynamic gym – with the right exercises, it can change and grow throughout your life. This ability of the brain to adapt and form new connections is called neuroplasticity. Think of it like muscle memory for your brain. Just like your muscles get stronger with use, your brain builds new pathways and strengthens existing ones based on your experiences, thoughts, and feelings.

### The Science of Neuroplasticity

This brain plasticity isn't just a scientific curiosity – it's a key to personal growth and mental well-being. Knowing our brains can change based on what we do and how we think gives us a powerful tool for self-improvement and recovery. Studies have shown that practices like mindfulness and meditation can actually change the structure of the brain, impacting areas related to focus, managing emotions, and self-awareness. This blows away the myth that we're stuck with certain behaviors or emotional responses – it opens doors for healing and positive change.

## Harnessing Neuroplasticity

So, how can you tap into this brainpower boost? Here are some strategies:

**Practice Makes Progress:** Similar to learning an instrument or a language, consistently engaging in positive mental habits can rewire your brain for better mental health. Find activities that align with your goals and make them a regular part of your routine.

**Skill Up!:** Learning new things isn't just good for life in general, it also promotes brain growth. Whether it's a new hobby, a different course of study, or even a new way to exercise, challenging yourself keeps your brain firing on all cylinders.

**Socialize and Connect:** Meaningful social interaction is a brain booster too. Conversations, especially those where you share and solve problems together, can create new neural pathways, making your brain more flexible.

**Challenge Yourself:** Regularly engaging your brain with puzzles, reading, or other mentally stimulating activities can help prevent cognitive decline and keep your brain growing.

## Mindfulness and Neuroplasticity

Mindfulness practices are particularly powerful when it comes to neuroplasticity. By focusing on the present moment without judgment, we can actually change the way our brains function and are structured. Areas of the brain involved in mindfulness and meditation are linked to focus, managing emotions, and self-awareness – all crucial for mental well-being. Over time, mindfulness can even reduce the brain's stress and anxiety response, making it a valuable ally in mental health recovery and resilience.

**Real-life Applications**

Here are some ways to put neuroplasticity into practice in your daily life:

**Meditation Matters:** Set aside some time each day for mindful meditation, focusing on your breath or bodily sensations. This strengthens brain areas vital for mindfulness and emotional regulation.

**Gratitude Boost:** Regularly writing down things you're grateful for can retrain your brain to notice and appreciate the positive aspects of life, fundamentally changing your outlook.

**Positive Affirmations:** Repeating positive affirmations can influence the neural pathways linked to self-esteem and positive thinking. Over time, this can transform the way you see yourself.

**Embrace Curiosity:** Make time each week to learn something new or explore a topic that interests you. This not only broadens your knowledge but also keeps your brain actively engaged and growing.

Understanding and using neuroplasticity is a testament to the amazing potential of our brains to change and grow. By incorporating practices that promote neural development, we can significantly impact our mental health and well-being. Whether it's mindfulness, learning new skills, or simply fostering positive mental habits, each step is a move towards a healthier and more fulfilling life.

## 3.7 Diet and Mental Health: A Personalized Nutrition Plan

We often think of diet as just about physical health, but it turns out what we eat has a big impact on our mental well-being too. A growing body of research shows a clear link between diet and mental health. This means what you put on your plate can actually help or hurt your mood, focus, and overall mental state.

## Nutrition's Impact on Mental Health

The brain is like a high-performance engine that needs the right fuel to run smoothly. It relies on a constant supply of vitamins, minerals, and other nutrients to function at its best. For example, omega-3 fatty acids, found in fatty fish and nuts, are known to support brain function and have been linked with lower levels of depression. Antioxidants in fruits and vegetables fight off damage that can affect mood and mental clarity. On the other hand, diets high in processed foods and sugary drinks have been associated with increased anxiety and depression symptoms. This highlights the importance of food as a key player in mental health – it can either support us or hold us back.

## Creating a Mental Health-Friendly Diet

With so much conflicting nutrition advice out there, it's easy to feel overwhelmed. The goal isn't to follow a one-size-fits-all plan, but to create a personalized approach that fits your needs and lifestyle. Here are some starting points:

**Focus on Whole Foods:** Make whole foods like fruits, vegetables, whole grains, lean protein, and healthy fats the foundation of your diet. These foods are packed with a wide range of nutrients essential for mental health.

**Incorporate Omega-3s:** Include sources of omega-3 fatty acids, like salmon, flaxseeds, or walnuts, in your meals to give your brain a boost.

**Limit Processed Foods:** Processed foods often contain additives and high amounts of sugar, which can negatively affect mood and energy levels. Try to cut back on these.

Stay Hydrated: Don't underestimate the power of water. It's crucial for all bodily functions, including brain function.

## Mindful Eating Practices

Mindful eating bridges the gap between nutrition and mental health, transforming each meal into an opportunity to enhance your well-being. Here's how to practice it:

**Distraction-Free Dining:** Put away your phone and other distractions while you eat. Focus on the experience of enjoying your food.

**Listen to Your Body:** Pay attention to your hunger and fullness cues. Eat when you're truly hungry and stop when you're comfortably full.

**Savor Every Bite:** Take the time to appreciate the taste and texture of your food. This makes eating more enjoyable and helps prevent overeating.

## Monitoring and Adjusting

Just like any aspect of your health, your diet's impact on your mental well-being needs ongoing attention and adjustments. Try keeping a food and mood diary for a few weeks to track what you eat and how you feel afterwards. See if you can identify patterns – which foods make you feel good and which ones seem to bring you down. Remember, it may take some time for dietary changes to show effects on your mental health. Be patient with yourself and find what works best for you.

As you learn more about your body's responses, you might need to make adjustments. Perhaps dairy makes you feel sluggish, or a protein-rich breakfast keeps your mood stable throughout the day. Use these insights to personalize your diet, focusing on balance and variety.

If you have specific health concerns or dietary restrictions, consider consulting with a registered dietitian or nutritionist. They can provide personalized advice and support to ensure your nutrition plan aligns with your overall health goals, including mental well-being.

This exploration of the connection between diet and mental health highlights the power of food to nourish not just our bodies, but also our minds. By being mindful of what we eat, prioritizing nutrient-rich foods, and listening to our bodies, we can create a foundation for mental well-being that supports us through life's challenges. After all, food sustains life, and with a mindful approach, each meal can be an opportunity to enhance its quality.

## 3.8 Building Resilience: Strategies That Work for You

We often hear about resilience as bouncing back from hardship. But it's more than just that. It's about growing through challenges, not just getting past them. Resilience isn't something you're born with – it's built over time through experiences and effort. Just like a muscle you strengthen with exercise, resilience develops as you navigate life's ups and downs. Here, we'll explore ways to build your resilience, adapt strategies to your unique situation, learn from setbacks, and find inspiration from those who've mastered this valuable skill.

### Cultivating Your Resilience

Think of resilience as a garden that needs constant care to flourish. Your background, experiences, and environment all play a role, just like soil, seeds, and weather affect real gardens. Here are some tailored strategies to cultivate your resilience garden:

**Mindset Matters:** A growth mindset is key. It means believing you can learn from all experiences, even the tough ones. Seeing challenges as opportunities to grow, not roadblocks, is crucial.

**Self-Care is Essential:** Regular self-care is the water and sunlight for your resilience garden. Taking care of yourself physically, mentally, and emotionally strengthens your ability to cope.

**Strong Connections are Key:** Just like plants in a garden support each other, strong and positive relationships do the same for us. Build connections that provide encouragement and understanding.

**Be Flexible:** Life throws curveballs. Develop flexible thinking, like adaptable garden soil that adjusts to changing weather. Practice seeing situations from different angles and finding creative solutions.

### Adapting Strategies to Fit Your Life

Not every strategy will fit perfectly. The key is finding what works for you and integrating it into your life. Here's how to personalize your approach:

**Try It Out, Reflect on It:** Experiment with different resilience-building practices and reflect on how they impact you. Keep what works and adjust or discard what doesn't.

**Make it a Habit:** Link new resilience practices to existing habits. For example, practice gratitude while having your morning coffee.

**Seek Feedback:** Sometimes, an outside perspective can be helpful. Talk to trusted friends or mentors about your strategies and be open to suggestions.

### Learning from Setbacks

Setbacks are inevitable, but each one offers a valuable lesson. When faced with failure, consider these actions:

**Reframe the Experience:** Instead of seeing setbacks as failures, see them as learning experiences. Ask yourself, "What can I learn from this?"

**Be Kind to Yourself:** Treat yourself with compassion during tough times. Acknowledge your efforts and remember that growth often comes from challenges.

**Don't Go It Alone:** Reach out to your support network. Sharing your experiences can provide comfort and new perspectives.

**Resilience in Action**

Seeing how others build resilience can be motivating. Here are a few examples:

**Maya:** After a career setback, Maya started a blog to share her journey of self-discovery and resilience. Writing became an outlet, and the support from readers boosted her strength.

**Eli:** Following a health diagnosis, Eli took up marathon running. The physical challenge and the supportive running community helped him build resilience and stay positive.

**Tara:** Volunteering with underprivileged youth taught Tara resilience through adversity. Witnessing the hope and determination of those she helped inspired her.

These stories highlight how resilience is about bouncing back, growing, and finding meaning in challenges. Maya found healing in expression and community, Eli in pushing his limits and finding support, and Tara in serving others and seeing their strength.

Building resilience is a personal, ongoing process. It requires patience, a willingness to learn, and the ability to adapt. Whether you're nurturing your mindset, connecting with others, learning from setbacks, or finding inspiration, each step you take strengthens your resilience and helps you bounce back stronger.

### 3.9 The Importance of Personal Boundaries in Mental Health

In mental health, setting and upholding personal boundaries plays a pivotal role, much like the banks of a river that guide its flow. These invisible lines we draw around our emotional, physical, and mental spaces ensure we navigate life's waters without losing ourselves to the currents of others' demands and expectations.

### Boundaries for well-being

Think of personal boundaries as the protective gear worn by athletes; without them, the risk of injury skyrockets. Similarly, without clear boundaries, our mental and emotional well-being is left vulnerable to the whims and wills of those around us. These boundaries are not walls but filters that allow healthy, nurturing relationships to flourish while keeping distressing and draining interactions at bay.

### Identifying boundary needs

Recognizing where boundaries are needed is akin to identifying weak points in a fortress. This process begins with a keen observation of feelings and reactions in various situations:

Note moments when you feel discomfort, resentment, or depletion after interactions. These are indicators that a boundary may have been crossed.

Reflect on relationships or situations where you consistently find yourself overextended or undervalued. These patterns signal areas where firmer boundaries could protect your well-being.

### Practical steps to set boundaries

Establishing and communicating these boundaries involves a blend of introspection and action. Here's how you can begin:

Clearly define what is acceptable and not in different areas of your life, be it work, relationships, or personal time.

Practice stating your boundaries out loud to yourself or a trusted friend's company. This rehearsal builds confidence in your ability to assert them when necessary.

Choose an appropriate time and setting to discuss your boundaries with those involved. Approach the conversation with clarity and assertiveness, focusing on your needs rather than placing blame.

Be prepared for pushback. Not everyone will respond positively to your boundaries initially. Stand firm, and remember that your well-being is the priority.

**Respecting your boundaries**

The final and often most challenging step is to honor the boundaries you've set for yourself. This act of self-respect is crucial for maintaining your mental health. Consider these strategies:

Regularly review your boundaries to ensure they still align with your needs. Life changes, and so too might your boundaries.

Pay attention to instances where you might be tempted to bend your rules. Pause and remind yourself why these boundaries were set in the first place.

Celebrate the moments when you successfully uphold your boundaries. Acknowledging these victories, no matter how small, reinforces this practice's importance for your well-being.

In the tapestry of mental health, personal boundaries are the threads that maintain the integrity of our emotional fabric, ensuring we remain whole and undamaged by external pressures. By identifying where these boundaries are needed, taking practical steps to establish and communicate them, and, most importantly, respecting them, we fortify our mental and emotional well-being, allowing us to navigate life's complexities with a sense of security and self-assuredness.

## 3.10 Choosing the Right Mental Health Professional for You

Finding the right mental health professional is like searching for a new house. You're looking for that perfect fit—a place where you feel safe, supported, and understood. Like any good house hunt, it requires understanding the landscape, knowing what you're looking for, inspecting thoroughly, and knowing if the chemistry is right.

**Navigating the options**

The world of mental health professionals is rich and varied, each with their areas of expertise. Here's a brief overview to help you start:

**Psychiatrists**: These are medical doctors specializing in diagnosing and treating mental health disorders, often through medication. They can be a go-to if you suspect your issues might have a biochemical component.

**Psychologists**: Holding advanced degrees in psychology, they focus on psychotherapy and treating emotional and mental suffering through behavioral intervention.

**Licensed Clinical Social Workers (LCSWs)**: With a focus on psychotherapy, they bring a broad perspective, often considering the impact of your environment and social factors on your mental health.

**Marriage and Family Therapists (MFTs)**: Specialized in relationship dynamics, they're ideal if your concerns are about family or romantic relationships.

**Licensed Professional Counselors (LPCs)**: They provide therapeutic support for various issues, from anxiety and depression to stress and life transitions.

Knowing the specialties and approaches of these professionals can help you narrow your search to those most likely to meet your needs.

**Finding a good fit**

The key to a successful therapeutic relationship is compatibility. Here's what to consider when looking for a mental health professional:

**Approach and Philosophy**: Does their therapeutic approach align with your preferences and beliefs? Some may lean towards cognitive behavioral therapy, while others prioritize psychoanalytic methods.

**Specializations**: Are they experienced in dealing with your specific issues? Expertise in areas relevant to your needs is crucial.

**Personality and Style**: Do you feel comfortable with their personality and communication style? It's essential that you feel understood and respected.

**Logistics**: Consider location, availability, and whether they accept your insurance. These practical matters can significantly impact your therapy experience.

**The Consultation Process**

Initial consultations are your opportunity to assess the fit. Think of it like test-driving a car—checking how it feels, asking questions, and seeing if it meets your needs. During this phase:

**Prepare Questions**: Come with a list of questions or concerns. Ask about their experience with your issues, their therapeutic approach, and what a typical session might look like.

**Share Openly**: Be as open as possible about what you're going through and what you hope to gain from therapy. This helps them understand your needs and determine if they can meet them.

**Assess Your Comfort Level**: Consider how you feel during the consultation. Do you feel heard and understood? Are you comfortable with their responses and demeanor?

**Discuss Expectations**: Talk about your goals and what you expect from therapy. This ensures you're both on the same page and working towards the same outcomes.

**Building a therapeutic relationship**

The foundation of effective therapy is a strong, trusting relationship with your mental health professional. It's a partnership where both parties contribute to the process. To foster this relationship:

**Be an Active Participant**: Engage actively in your sessions. The more effort you put into treatment, the more benefit you will gain from it.

**Communicate**: If something isn't working for you, speak up. Your feedback is crucial whether it's the pace, approach, or even the session time.

**Trust the Process**: Therapy can sometimes be challenging. Trust in the expertise of your mental health professional, and the process can lead to breakthroughs and significant progress.

**Commitment**: Like any meaningful change, therapy requires time and commitment. Be patient with yourself and the process, and celebrate the small victories.

Selecting the right mental health professional is critical to healing and growth. Finding that perfect match requires a mix of research, introspection, and trial. But once you do, the journey towards a healthier, more fulfilled life becomes a shared venture—one where you're supported, guided, and understood, ready to tackle whatever challenges come your way.

## 3.11 Creating Your Own Mental Health Support Network

A robust support network acts much like a lighthouse, offering guidance and illumination through the stormy seas of life's challenges. It's not merely about having people around; it's about fostering connections that bring real value to your mental health journey. This nurturing circle can significantly bolster your resilience, offering perspectives, encouragement, and understanding when needed.

### The Value of Support

Imagine navigating a labyrinth with no map or compass; the journey feels daunting. Now, picture the same scenario with a guide by your side, offering directions and reassurance. This is the essence of a support network's value—it provides guidance, reduces feelings of isolation, and enhances your ability to cope with life's stressors. In moments of doubt, these connections remind you of your strengths and progress, propelling you forward.

### Identifying Potential Support

Finding and recognizing those who can be part of your support network involves both introspection and observation:

Look to those already in your life who have shown empathy, understanding, or shared experiences. These individuals often form the core of your support circle.

Expand your view to include coworkers, acquaintances, or members of clubs and organizations you're part of. Support can come from unexpected sources, growing from shared interests or goals.

Consider professionals who can provide support, such as therapists, counselors, or life coaches. Their expertise can be invaluable in navigating specific challenges.

## Engaging with Support Groups

Both formal and informal support groups offer unique benefits. Here's how to engage with them effectively:

Research groups that align with your needs, whether focused on specific mental health issues, life changes, or general wellness.

Attend a few sessions with an open mind. Initial discomfort is normal, but regular attendance can help gauge the group's fit.

Participate actively. Sharing your experiences can be therapeutic and foster deeper connections within the group.

Respect confidentiality. Trust is the foundation of these groups, and respecting each member's privacy encourages openness and honesty.

## Nurturing Your Network

Maintaining and nurturing your support network requires effort and intentionality:

Regular check-ins keep connections strong. A simple message, call, or meeting for coffee can keep the lines of communication open.

Offer support to others. The strength of your network lies in reciprocity; being there for others fosters a culture of mutual support.

Celebrate successes together. Acknowledging milestones and achievements reinforces the positive impact of your support network.

Be mindful of boundaries. Healthy relationships respect each person's limits and capacities.

In creating and nurturing your mental health support network, you weave a safety net that not only catches you in times of fall but also lifts you toward growth and healing. This network, built on the pillars of empathy, understanding, and mutual support, becomes a cornerstone of your mental wellness, illuminating paths through the darkest tunnels and offering solace in moments of solitude.

With these strategies, you can cultivate a support network that resonates with your unique journey, offering a blend of camaraderie, wisdom, and compassion. As you move forward, remember that this network is not static but evolves as you do, adapting to your changing needs and circumstances. It stands as a testament to the power of connection in our lives, underscoring the profound truth that we thrive not in isolation but in the company of others who understand, support, and uplift us.

As we wrap up this exploration of constructing your mental health support network, we're reminded of the profound impact of human connection on our well-being. From pinpointing potential allies to engaging with groups and nurturing these relationships, each step enriches our lives, providing comfort, understanding, and strength. This foundational network supports us through challenges and amplifies our joys, highlighting the shared nature of our human experience. As we transition to the next chapter, let's carry forward the invaluable insights gained here, ready to apply them in cultivating a life marked by resilience, growth, and profound connection.

# Chapter 4: Shedding Light on Mental Health Mysteries

Stepping into the mental health conversation can sometimes feel like entering a maze at night without a flashlight. You know there's a way through, but the path isn't clear, and wrong turns seem inevitable. This chapter is about switching on that flashlight, not by providing a map, but by illuminating the space around us, making the journey less daunting and the direction a bit clearer.

In today's world, where mental health information is as plentiful as the stars in the night sky, distinguishing between helpful guidance and misleading advice is more crucial than ever. It's about sifting through the noise to find the melodies that resonate with truth and understanding. Here, we address the questions that often linger in the shadows, clarify common misconceptions, and offer practical advice rooted in reality.

**Clarifying Misconceptions**

Misconceptions about mental health are like weeds in a garden; they can take root and spread if not addressed. Here are truths to counteract common myths:

"People with mental health issues can't handle work or school." Reality: Countless individuals with mental health conditions are thriving in their careers and academics. It's not about the condition but how it's managed.

"Therapy and self-help are wastes of time. "Just get out of it." Reality: Mental health issues are caused by intricate interactions between the brain, environment, and experiences. Effective treatment, such as therapy, targets the root causes.

"Only a few kinds of people have mental health issues." Reality: Mental health issues do not discriminate. They may affect anybody, irrespective of age, gender, or background.

## FAQs

In the spirit of shedding light on mental health, let's tackle some Frequently Asked Questions:

What's the difference between feeling sad and being depressed? Sadness is a normal emotion we all feel at times. Depression, however, is a clinical condition characterized by persistent sadness, loss of interest, and other symptoms that significantly impact daily functioning.

Can exercise help with mental health? Yes. Exercise releases endorphins, known as 'feel-good' hormones, which can improve mood and decrease anxiety. Regular physical activity has been shown to positively affect mental health.

How do I know if I should see a therapist? If you're struggling with your emotions, thoughts, or behaviors to a point where it's affecting your daily life, seeking a therapist can be beneficial. It's about getting support, not about reaching a crisis point.

## Sources of Misinformation

In the digital age, misinformation about mental health is rampant. So, where does it often originate?

**Social Media**: Platforms can breed myths, especially when non-experts present opinions as facts.

**Movies and TV**: Entertainment media often portray mental health conditions inaccurately, leading to stereotypes and misconceptions.

**Word of Mouth**: Sometimes, well-meaning advice from friends or family can perpetuate myths due to a lack of accurate information.

To combat misinformation, always seek out reputable sources. Websites of established mental health organizations, peer-reviewed journals, and consultations with healthcare professionals are good starting points.

**4.1 The Importance of Education**

Understanding mental health isn't just beneficial; it's necessary for creating supportive communities and promoting well-being. Education can play a pivotal role in this by:

**Breaking down stigma**: Knowledge fosters understanding, reducing the stigma that often surrounds mental health issues and making it easier for individuals to seek help.

**Promoting early intervention**: Recognizing the signs of mental health conditions can lead to earlier intervention, improving outcomes.

**Encouraging empathy**: Learning about mental health can increase empathy towards those experiencing mental health challenges, fostering a more inclusive society.

**Visual Element: Infographic on Common Mental Health Misconceptions and Facts**

This chapter includes an infographic summarizing critical misconceptions about mental health alongside factual counterpoints. It serves as a visual reminder of the truths that can help dispel myths and foster a more informed understanding of mental health.

**Interactive Element**: Quiz on Distinguishing Mental Health Facts from Fiction

Engage with a quiz to test your ability to distinguish between common mental health myths and realities. This interactive tool reinforces your understanding and challenges misconceptions you may hold.

**Textual Element**: Checklist for Finding Reliable Mental Health Information

A handy checklist to guide you in assessing the reliability of mental health information sources. It includes tips on evaluating the credibility of websites, identifying reputable authors, and spotting red flags that suggest misinformation.

In this age, where information and misinformation are just a click away, becoming discerning consumers of mental health information is not just beneficial—it's crucial. By clarifying misconceptions, answering common questions, highlighting sources of misinformation, and emphasizing the role of education, we're not just navigating the maze more effectively; we're also contributing to a world where mental health is understood, not feared. Through education and awareness, we can all play a part in illuminating the path forward, ensuring no one has to navigate the complexities of mental health in the dark.

## 4.2 Overcoming Isolation: Strategies for Building Connection

Much like a shadow, isolation can grow longer and more imposing as the sun sets. This shadow can stretch out in our lives due to various circumstances—moving to a new city, experiencing a transition in life, or facing challenges that make us retreat inward. The impact on mental health is tangible, often leading to feelings of loneliness, increased stress, and a dip in overall well-being. Recognizing the signs of isolation is the first step towards inviting more light into our lives.

### Breaking the cycle of isolation

Understanding the cycle of isolation begins with acknowledging how easily it can spiral. What starts as a quiet evening alone can quickly turn into days, then weeks of limited interaction, impacting our mental health significantly. Breaking this cycle requires intentional action:

**Acknowledge the feelings**: Recognizing the sense of isolation is crucial. It's okay to admit to feeling lonely or disconnected.

**Small steps**: Reaching out doesn't have to be a grand gesture. A simple text message, a comment on a friend's social media post, or even making small talk with a neighbor can be meaningful.

**Routine involvement**: Creating a routine that involves social interaction, even in the most minor ways, can slowly rebuild the bridge to connectivity.

**Building bridges**

For those who find themselves on the introverted side of the spectrum or grappling with social anxiety, initiating and maintaining connections poses its own set of challenges. Here are some tips for building those bridges, plank by plank:

**Shared interests**: Engaging in activities or hobbies you're genuinely interested in can naturally lead to connections with like-minded individuals.

**Volunteer**: Offering your time to causes you care about can enrich your sense of purpose and introduce you to a community with shared values.

Be open about your feelings: Sometimes, just sharing that you're trying to be more social or overcome feelings of isolation can open doors. People are often more understanding and willing to connect than we might expect.

**Leveraging technology**

While it's true that digital platforms can contribute to a sense of isolation, when used mindfully, they can also be powerful tools for fostering connections:

Selectivity is critical: Choose platforms and communities that align with your interests and values. It's better to have meaningful interactions in one or two groups than to spread yourself thin across many.

**Set boundaries**: Limit your time online to ensure that digital interactions complement, rather than replace, real-world connections.

**Engage in positive interactions**: Use your online presence to support others, share interests, and engage in discussions that uplift rather than drain.

**Community involvement**

Becoming active in your local community can provide a sense of belonging and connection that's hard to replicate in digital spaces. Here's how you can immerse yourself in community activities:

**Local events and clubs**: Look for community centers, libraries, or local groups that host events, workshops, or clubs that pique your interest.

**Take a class**: Learning something new, be it a language, a craft, or a dance, can not only enrich your skill set but also introduce you to people who share your enthusiasm for learning.

**Offer your skills**: If you have a particular skill or expertise, consider offering a workshop or a class in your community. Teaching is a profound way to connect with others and share your passion.

In navigating the complex terrain of mental health, understanding the profound impact of isolation is crucial. However, recognizing it is just the first step. By deliberately breaking the cycle, building bridges of connection, wisely using technology, and immersing ourselves in community life, we foster a sense of belonging that illuminates our lives. These strategies are not quick fixes but gradual steps towards a more prosperous, connected existence. Through intentional effort, we can transform the shadow of isolation into a path that leads us back to warmth, companionship and shared humanity.

## 4.3 Accessing Professional Help: Navigating the Barriers

Opening the door to professional mental health support can sometimes feel like trying to unlock a door with the wrong key. You know help is on the other side, but reaching it isn't as straightforward as it should be. This complexity doesn't stem from a lack of desire or recognition of the need for support but often from tangible barriers that stand in the way. Identifying these barriers is the first step toward unlocking the door to mental health care.

### Identifying Barriers

Several obstacles can hinder access to mental health care, making it crucial to recognize and address them:

**Stigma**: The shadow of stigma looms large, deterring many from seeking the help they need. The fear of judgment from others or self can be paralyzing.

**Cost**: Financial resources, or the lack thereof, significantly impact one's ability to access mental health services. High costs and inadequate insurance coverage can be prohibitive.

**Lack of Resources**: In many areas, mainly rural or underserved communities, there is a stark scarcity of mental health professionals, which can limit access to care.

**Awareness**: Sometimes, the obstacle is not knowing where to start or what resources are available.

### Solutions to Common Barriers

For every barrier, solutions and workarounds exist that can help pave the way to accessing the care needed:

**Sliding Scale Fees**: Many therapists offer sliding scale fees based on income, making therapy more affordable for those with financial constraints.

**Online Therapy Options**: Teletherapy has risen in prominence, offering a flexible and often more affordable alternative to traditional in-person sessions.

**Community Resources**: Local community centers, nonprofit organizations, and support groups often provide mental health services at reduced rates or even for free.

**Education**: Increasing one's understanding of mental health issues and the types of help available can demystify seeking care.

### Advocating for Oneself

Navigating the healthcare system to get the support you need requires self-advocacy. Here are some ways to champion your mental health within the healthcare system:

**Preparation**: Before appointments, prepare a list of concerns and questions. Knowing what you want to address beforehand can help you maximize your time.

**Persistence**: If you're not getting the answers or support you need, don't hesitate to ask again or seek a second opinion. Your well-being is worth advocating for.

**Insurance Navigation**: Learn the specifics of your insurance coverage for mental health services. Contact your provider for a list of covered therapists or ask about out-of-network reimbursement rates if necessary.

**Self-Education**: Familiarize yourself with your rights as a patient and the standards of care you should expect. Being informed can empower you to advocate more effectively.

**Alternative Resources**

When traditional paths to mental health support are blocked, alternative and supplementary resources can provide valuable support:

**Digital Apps**: Numerous mental health apps offer tools for self-care, stress management, and mood tracking, providing a supplementary resource for managing mental health.

**Online Support Groups**: These groups offer a platform for sharing experiences and receiving support from others who understand what you're going through, breaking down feelings of isolation.

**Educational Content**: Podcasts, books, and online courses about mental health can offer insights and coping strategies, increasing your toolkit for managing mental health challenges.

**Mindfulness and Meditation**: While not a substitute for professional help, incorporating mindfulness and meditation into your daily routine can improve mental well-being and resilience.

Navigating the barriers to accessing mental health care might seem daunting, but solutions and paths forward exist. By identifying the obstacles, exploring solutions, advocating for oneself, and leveraging alternative resources, the door to support becomes easier to unlock.

## 4.4 Managing Information Overload: A Guide to Selective Engagement

We often find ourselves drowning in endless notifications, updates, and information in this digital age. It feels like standing in the middle of a bustling city intersection, with signs pointing everywhere. How do we navigate this intersection without losing our way? The key lies in becoming selective in what we engage with and how we consume information.

### Selective Consumption

Selective consumption is akin to being a discerning diner at a buffet filled with various dishes. Not everything on offer will suit your liking or your health. Apply similar discernment to the information you consume:

Start by identifying what truly matters to you. What aligns with your values, interests, and goals? This clarity will help you filter out the noise.

Prioritize quality over quantity. Choose sources that provide value and enrich your understanding rather than those that simply add to the clutter.

Learn to say no. You don't have to read every article or watch every video that comes your way. If it doesn't serve you, let it go.

### Curating Your Feed

Social media and news feeds are often the biggest culprits in overwhelming us with information. However, they also offer tools to tailor what you see:

Use the 'unfollow' or 'mute' feature liberally. This allows you to remain connected with friends or contacts while minimizing exposure to stress-inducing content.

Subscribe or follow pages and channels that uplift you and contribute positively to your day. This could be accounts focused on mental health, personal growth, or hobbies you enjoy.

Set up filters or lists. Many platforms allow you to categorize your contacts or the type of content you see, helping you easily access what you find beneficial.

**Scheduled Disconnects**

Taking regular breaks from digital devices has been shown to profoundly impact mental wellness. Think of it as giving your mind a vacation, a chance to recharge and reset:

Plan short daily breaks where you step away from all screens. This might be during meals, the first hour after waking up, or before bedtime.

Consider a more extended disconnect, such as a digital detox weekend, where you significantly reduce or eliminate screen time. Notice the difference it makes in your stress levels and overall mood.

Make these disconnects a non-negotiable part of your routine, marking them in your calendar if needed. Treat this time as you would any necessary appointment.

**Mindful Media Consumption**

Approaching media consumption mindfully means being fully present and intentional with your engagement. This doesn't mean avoiding media but instead choosing to interact with it in ways that serve you:

Before opening an app or clicking on a link, pause momentarily. Is what I'm doing with my time right now the best use of it? Will my day be improved by this?

Be an active rather than a passive consumer. Engage with content by reflecting on it, discussing it with others, or using it as a springboard for further exploration.

Notice how different types of content affect your mood and energy levels. Use this awareness to make more informed choices about what to consume in the future.

In a world where information is endless, and the pressure to stay constantly connected looms large, managing information overload is not just about reducing stress; it's about reclaiming our mental space and ensuring that our engagement with digital content is meaningful and purposeful. By applying strategies of selective consumption, curating our feeds, scheduling disconnects, and approaching media consumption mindfully, we confidently navigate the bustling intersection of the digital age, ensuring that we keep moving in the direction that leads to our well-being and growth.

## 4.5 Skepticism and Hope: Balancing Realism with Optimism

In mental health, finding an equilibrium between skepticism and hope can feel like walking a tightrope. On one side, we're bombarded with quick fixes and miracle cures that promise the world but often deliver little. On the other hand, the genuine challenges we face require us not to lose sight of hope, which keeps us moving forward. This delicate balance is not about swinging wildly between extremes but about navigating the space between with grace and understanding.

### Developing a Healthy Level of Skepticism

Skepticism, in its most constructive form, is like a sieve, separating the chaff of empty promises from the wheat of genuine solutions. It invites us to question and critically evaluate the plethora of available mental health advice, therapies, and treatments. Here's how we can cultivate this skepticism without veering into cynicism:

**Research and verification**: Before embracing any mental health trend or treatment, dive into its background. Look for scientific studies, reviews from reputable health organizations, and feedback from individuals with firsthand experience.

**Recognizing red flags**: Be wary of any solution that claims to be a cure-all. Mental health is complex, and what works for one person might not work for another. Instant solutions rarely exist in this nuanced landscape.

**Seeking professional guidance**: When in doubt, turn to professionals. A conversation with a mental health practitioner can provide clarity and direct you toward treatments with a solid foundation in research and practice.

## Maintaining Hope and Optimism

While skepticism helps us navigate the sea of information, hope serves as our compass, guiding us through the fog of uncertainty. Here's how we can keep this light burning, even in the darkest times:

**Celebrating small victories**: Every step forward, no matter how modest, is a triumph. These moments are milestones worth acknowledging, whether it's a day when anxiety didn't hold you back or a session where you uncovered a deeper understanding of yourself.

**Connecting with stories of resilience**: There's immense power in hearing how others have navigated their mental health challenges. These narratives offer practical insights and remind us that we're not alone in our struggles.

**Cultivating a supportive network**: Surround yourself with individuals who uplift and encourage you. This circle can include friends, family, support groups, or online communities. Their belief in your journey can bolster your own.

## Setting Realistic and Achievable Goals

Goal setting acts as our roadmap, offering direction and a sense of purpose. However, these goals must be grounded in realism to prevent setting ourselves up for disappointment. Here are strategies for practical goal setting:

**Breaking down goals**: Large, overarching goals can be overwhelming. Divide them up into smaller, more doable assignments that you can do. This approach makes progress more tangible and less daunting.

**Adjusting expectations**: Be flexible in your expectations. If a goal proves too challenging, it's okay to reassess and adapt it. This isn't a setback but a recalibration based on a deeper understanding of your needs and capabilities.

**Celebrating progress**: Acknowledge every step forward, no matter how small. These celebrations reinforce the positive impact of your efforts and keep motivation high.

## Sharing Success Stories

Incorporating success stories into our narrative inspires and grounds our expectations in reality. Here are ways these stories can foster hope:

**Relatability**: Stories that resonate with our experiences remind us that our challenges are not insurmountable. They provide a mirror to our potential for growth and recovery.

**Learning from diversity**: Success comes in many forms and paths. By exploring various stories, we understand there's no single way to achieve mental wellness. This diversity encourages us to find the path that aligns with our unique circumstances.

**The power of resilience**: Hearing about others who have faced setbacks yet continued to strive towards their goals instills a sense of resilience. It's a reminder that while the journey may not be linear, perseverance is critical.

Navigating the world of mental health requires a delicate balance between skepticism and hope. By developing a healthy level of skepticism, we equip ourselves to discern the credible from the questionable. Maintaining hope and optimism ensures we don't lose sight of our potential for growth and healing. Setting realistic goals provides a clear sense of direction while engaging with success stories offers inspiration and a practical perspective on what can be achieved. This balance isn't about ignoring the complexities of mental health but about approaching them with a mindset that is both critical and hopeful, allowing us to navigate our paths with confidence and clarity.

## 4.6 Dealing with Burnout: Recognizing Signs and Taking Action

Burnout creeps up like a shadow at dusk, often unnoticed until the landscape of our well-being is dimmed. It's the culmination of stress, not just from a heavy workload but a balance that's lacking. Understanding this can transform how we address our energy reserves, ensuring we're not just scraping by but thriving.

### Signs of Burnout

Recognizing burnout requires a keen eye for its subtle and not-so-subtle signs. It's like watching for the first stars to appear in the evening sky; you must know where to look.

A sense of daily grind that feels insurmountable, where tasks once handled with ease now feel like mountains.

Emotional exhaustion blankets your days, making it hard to muster enthusiasm for what you once loved.

Feeling detached or cynical about work, where your job feels more like a sentence than a choice.

Noticeable decline in performance, where mistakes creep in, and the quality of work slips.

**Preventative Measures**

Preventing burnout isn't about avoiding hard work; it's about working smart and with intention. It's the art of balancing, not just juggling.

**Setting Boundaries**: Define clear lines between work and personal time. This might mean turning off email notifications after hours or dedicating a space solely for work to clock out once you step away mentally.

**Prioritizing Self-Care**: Incorporate activities that replenish your energy. Make these non-negotiable parts of your day, whether it's a hobby that brings joy, exercise to clear your mind, or simply quiet time to decompress.

**Managing Workload**: Learn to delegate and say no. Assess tasks' importance and urgency, and be realistic about what you can handle. It's not about doing less but doing what matters without overextending yourself.

**Recovery Strategies**

Finding your way back from burnout requires patience and proactive steps. Think of it as nurturing a garden back to health; it takes time, care, and the right conditions.

**Rest**: Allow yourself to step back and rest, truly rest. This might mean taking a break from work, a vacation, or just a weekend where you disconnect from all work-related tasks.

**Seek Support**: Talk to someone, whether a professional can guide you through recovery or confide in friends or family about how you're feeling.

**Reassess and Realign**: Use this time to reflect on what led to burnout. What needs to change? It might be aspects of your job, your approach to work, or even broader life choices.

**Creating a Sustainable Balance**

Sustaining a balance that keeps burnout at bay is like maintaining an equilibrium on a seesaw. It requires constant adjustment and awareness.

**Mindful Planning**: Plan your weeks and days with a balance in mind. Allocate time for work, rest, play, and relationships. It's not just about filling in slots in a calendar but ensuring harmony in how your time is spent.

**Flexibility**: Be prepared to adjust as you go. Some days require more from you, and others might offer a chance to slow down. Listen to what you need and be willing to shift your plans accordingly.

**Regular Check-ins**: Make it a habit to assess your well-being periodically. Are you feeling stretched thin, or is there a sense of balance? Use these check-ins to make necessary adjustments before signs of burnout reappear.

Recognizing and addressing burnout is pivotal in navigating the demands of work and life. It's about honoring our limits, nurturing our well-being, and making choices that sustain our productivity, happiness, and health. Through mindful strategies and proactive steps, we can guard against burnout, ensuring we're surviving and living.

## 4.7 Addressing Stigma: From Self-Judgment to Self-Compassion

At the core of many individuals' reluctance to seek mental health support or even engage in open conversations about their struggles lies a pervasive adversary: stigma. This insidious force shapes societal views and infiltrates our self-perception, often leaving us mired in self-judgment. To dismantle stigma, we must first understand its roots and its profound impact on those grappling with mental health challenges.

### Understanding stigma

Stigma is defined by the Oxford English Dictionary as a mark of disgrace connected to a certain situation, trait, or individual. When it comes to mental health, stigma manifests in several forms, including public stigma, the societal reaction that marginalizes individuals; self-stigma, the internalization of these negative perceptions; and institutional stigma, systemic policies or practices that limit opportunities for those with mental health conditions. The effects are far-reaching, deterring people from seeking help due to fear of judgment or discrimination and exacerbating feelings of isolation and worthlessness.

Dismantling stigma begins with education, fostering empathy, and creating spaces for open dialogue. By challenging the myths and misconceptions surrounding mental health, we can shift the narrative toward one of understanding and acceptance.

### Self-compassion exercises

A powerful antidote to self-stigma is self-compassion. This approach entails treating oneself with the same love, care, and support that one would provide to a close friend. Here are exercises to cultivate self-compassion:

**Mindfulness of Self-Talk**: Pay attention to your inner dialogue. When you notice self-critical thoughts, pause and ask yourself,

"Would I say this to someone I care about?" If not, strive to reframe the thought more compassionately and supportably.

**Self-Compassion Break**: Whenever you find yourself amid a problematic situation or overwhelmed by negative emotions, take a moment for a self-compassion break. Acknowledge your feelings ("This is hard right now"), remind yourself that you're not alone in your struggles ("Others feel this way too"), and offer yourself kindness ("May I be kind to myself in this moment").

**Gratitude Journal**: Each day, write down three things about yourself for which you're grateful. Focusing on your strengths and positive qualities can counterbalance tendencies toward self-criticism.

### Challenging societal stigma

Confronting and changing societal stigma requires collective effort and strategic action. Here are steps to challenge the stigma surrounding mental health in your community and beyond:

**Speak Up**: Use your voice to challenge stigma when you encounter it, whether in casual conversations, on social media, or in public forums. Sharing accurate information and personal experiences can help dispel myths and change perceptions.

**Support Mental Health Initiatives**: Participate in or support campaigns, events, and organizations dedicated to mental health awareness and advocacy. These platforms can amplify efforts to challenge stigma and promote a more inclusive society.

**Educate Others**: Offer to speak about mental health at schools, workplaces, or community centers. Education is a powerful tool for changing attitudes and fostering a more understanding community.

**Role models and allies**

Becoming a role model or ally in the fight against mental health stigma involves leading by example and offering support to those affected. Here's how you can make a difference:

**Share Your Story**: If you're comfortable, sharing your experiences with mental health challenges can be incredibly powerful. It humanizes the issue, breaks down barriers of isolation, and can inspire others to seek help or speak out.

**Offer Support**: Be an active listener and offer non-judgmental support to friends, family members, or colleagues struggling with mental health issues. Knowing someone is there to listen without judgment can make all the difference.

**Educate Yourself**: Continuously expand your understanding of mental health issues and the impact of stigma. The more informed you are, the better equipped you'll be to support others and advocate for change.

Through concerted efforts to understand stigma, practice self-compassion, challenge societal norms, and be role models of empathy and support, we can deconstruct the barriers that stigma erects. It's a journey from self-judgment to self-compassion, marginalization to inclusion, and silence to open dialogue. In doing so, we pave the way for a future where mental health is destigmatized, and seeking help is viewed not as a sign of weakness but as a step towards healing and strength.

## 4.8 Tailoring Exercises for High-Pressure Lifestyles

Living a life crammed with deadlines, meetings, and obligations often means our mental health takes a backseat. For those navigating the fast lanes of demanding careers or personal commitments, finding moments for mental health practices can feel like squeezing water from a stone. Yet, it's in these high-pressure environments that such practices are most needed. Let's explore how to weave mental wellness into the fabric of a bustling life, ensuring it strengthens rather than frays under stress.

**Adapting to High Stress**

High-pressure lifestyles demand a lot from us, often leaving little room for anything else. However, adapting mental health exercises to fit this whirlwind of activity is not only possible but critical. It involves identifying pockets of time and transforming them into opportunities for stress relief and mental fortification. This could mean using the first five minutes of your lunch break for deep breathing exercises or turning your commute into a time for a guided meditation through audio. The key is to find practices that are both effective and efficient, providing maximum benefit without requiring large chunks of time.

**Micro-practices**

Micro-practices are small, powerful exercises that can be seamlessly integrated into your day without disrupting your schedule. They are the mental health equivalent of taking the stairs instead of the elevator – small actions adding significant benefits. Consider incorporating the following into your routine:

Two-Minute Breathing Breaks Twice a day, pause for two minutes to focus solely on your breath. This can help center your thoughts and reduce stress.

**Gratitude Moments**: Think of one thing you're grateful for each evening. This simple act can shift your focus from the day's stresses to its blessings.

**Mindful Walking**: Use part of your walk to your next meeting or errand as a moment of mindfulness. Pay attention to the sensation of your feet touching the ground, the sounds around you, and the air on your skin.

### Prioritizing Self-Care

In a world that often glorifies busyness, claiming time for self-care can feel like a revolutionary act. Yet, it's essential for maintaining your mental and physical health amidst high pressure. Prioritizing self-care means recognizing its value and making it an untouchable part of your schedule. It means understanding that to perform at your best, you must feel your best. Start by identifying one non-negotiable self-care activity you can commit to daily, no matter how small. It could be a 10-minute walk, reading a book for pleasure, or simply enjoying a cup of tea in silence.

### Boundary Setting

Setting boundaries is critical in high-pressure environments to protect your mental health. It's about knowing your limits and communicating them effectively to others. Here are steps to establish and maintain these boundaries:

**Identify Your Non-Negotiables**: These are aspects of your life that you refuse to compromise on for work or other obligations, such as family time, sleep, or self-care practices.

**Communicate Clearly**: Whether it's with your boss, colleagues, or family, be clear about what you can and cannot do. It's not about being inflexible but ensuring you can meet your commitments without sacrificing your well-being.

**Learn to Say No**: This is often the most challenging and freeing. Saying no to additional responsibilities that would stretch you too thin preserves your energy for the tasks and people most important to you.

**Regular Reviews**: As life changes, so too will your boundaries. Make it a habit to regularly assess whether your current boundaries still serve you or if adjustments are needed.

Incorporating mental health practices into a high-pressure lifestyle is not about adding more to your plate but stirring some well-deserved self-care into the mix. By adapting exercises to fit the rhythms of your day, embracing micro-practices for their convenience and impact, prioritizing self-care as a non-negotiable part of your routine, and setting clear boundaries to protect your time and energy, you create a life that not only demands but respects and replenishes your mental well-being.

## 4.9 Finding Community: How to Connect with Others on Your Journey

In the vast landscape of mental health, the presence of a community that echoes our thoughts, struggles, and victories can be a beacon of light. The sense of belonging, understanding, and shared growth from connecting with those who tread a similar path is invaluable. It's about creating a space where vulnerabilities are met with empathy, and every shared story becomes a stitch in the fabric of a supportive network.

### Seeking Like-minded Individuals

The quest for companionship on this path begins with looking in the right places. Here are strategies to help you find those who resonate with your experiences or aspirations:

**Interest-based Activities**: Engage in activities aligned with your interests, whether art classes, hiking groups, or book clubs. These settings naturally foster connections with individuals who share common ground.

**Social Media Platforms**: Platforms like Instagram, Twitter, and Facebook host numerous communities centered around mental health and wellness. Search for hashtags related to your interests or experiences to find these groups.

Workshops and Seminars: Attend workshops, talks, or seminars on topics relevant to your mental health journey. These events expand your knowledge and connect you with others who are similarly invested in their well-being.

### Support Groups and Forums

Digital or local support groups and forums provide a platform for exchanging experiences, advice, and encouragement. To make the most of these communities:

**Do Your Research**: Look for groups explicitly addressing your interest or concern. Whether it's managing anxiety, navigating depression, or discussing therapy techniques, the right group can offer tailored support.

**Be an Active Participant**: While it's okay to observe initially, active participation increases the benefits you'll receive. Ask questions, talk about your experiences, and help others.

**Ensure a Safe Environment**: Opt for communities that prioritize the safety and privacy of their members. Moderated forums or groups with clear guidelines are often more conducive to open and respectful conversations.

### Creating Your Community

Sometimes, the exact community we're searching for doesn't exist yet. In such cases, consider starting your own. Here's how:

**Identify the Purpose**: Determine what you want your community to achieve. Is it a support network for people with specific mental health challenges, a group focused on wellness activities, or a forum for sharing resources?

**Choose Your Platform**: Depending on your comfort and the nature of the community, decide whether it will be online (like a Facebook group or a subreddit) or in-person (meet-ups, coffee chats).

**Spread the Word**: Use your social networks, both online and offline, to invite people to join. Engage with local organizations, wellness centers, or therapists who can help promote your community to those who might benefit from it.

**The Power of Shared Experiences**

The magic of finding or creating a community lies in the power of shared experiences. When we open up about our struggles, achievements, and learnings, we lighten our load and pave the way for others to do the same. Consider these points:

**Validation and Normalization**: Hearing others voice thoughts or feelings we've quietly harbored can validate our experiences and normalize what we're going through.

**Collective Wisdom**: Communities bring together a wealth of knowledge and strategies. From coping mechanisms to recommendations for professional help, the shared wisdom of the group can be a rich resource.

**Empathy and Support**: In a community, empathy flows freely. Members quickly offer support, understanding, and encouragement, fostering an environment where everyone feels seen and heard.

In the journey of mental health, the community search is a step towards not just healing and growth but also towards breaking down the walls of isolation that often accompany our struggles. Whether through finding like-minded individuals, engaging in support groups and forums, creating your community, or embracing the power of shared experiences, the connections we forge can illuminate our path and inspire continued progress. In this shared space, every story, every voice, and every silence finds a resonance, weaving together a tapestry of collective strength and hope.

### 4.10 Embracing Neurodiversity in Mental Health Strategies

In a world teeming with diverse minds, neurodiversity is a testament to the vast spectrum of human cognition. This concept, rooted in the understanding that neurological differences are to be recognized and respected as any other human variation, shifts the narrative from deficit to diversity. It acknowledges that brains work differently, and these differences include but are not limited to autism, ADHD, dyslexia, and more. In mental health, embracing neurodiversity implies crafting strategies that honor these unique neural landscapes, ensuring that every individual has access to care that genuinely reflects their needs.

#### Personalized Strategies

Tailoring mental health care to accommodate neurodivergent individuals isn't just a courtesy; it's a necessity. The one-size-fits-all approach falls short of addressing the nuanced needs of those whose brains process information in distinctive ways. Personalization begins with listening—an earnest effort to understand the individual's experiences, challenges, and preferences. From there, strategies might include:

**Adaptable Communication Methods**: Traditional talk therapy might be daunting or ineffective for some. Alternatives like written communication, art therapy, or the use of technology can offer meaningful pathways to expression and understanding.

**Environment Consideration**: People with neurodivergent traits frequently experience sensory sensitivity. A therapy setting that allows for control over sensory inputs—like lighting, sound, and seating arrangements—can significantly affect comfort and focus.

Strengths-Based Approach: Focusing on the individual's strengths and interests can foster engagement and efficacy in therapy. This approach leverages what the individual excels at, building confidence and skills contributing to their well-being.

**Advocacy and Acceptance**

Navigating a world designed for neurotypical minds can be challenging for neurodivergent individuals. Advocacy becomes a tool for carving out space where their needs are recognized and met. This advocacy extends into seeking acceptance, advocating not just for accommodation but for celebrating neurodiversity. Strategies include:

**Self-Advocacy Training**: Empowering neurodivergent individuals with the skills to advocate for themselves in personal, educational, and professional settings is crucial. This might involve role-playing scenarios, developing communication strategies, or understanding legal rights.

**Community Advocacy**: Joining or forming groups that push for systemic changes in how neurodiversity is understood and accommodated can amplify individual voices, driving societal and policy-level changes.

**Educational Initiatives**: Offering workshops or resources about neurodiversity to employers, educators, and healthcare providers can foster more inclusive and supportive environments.

**Supporting Neurodivergent Individuals**

Creating a supportive environment for neurodivergent friends, family members, or colleagues involves intentional actions and an open heart. It's about making space for differences and offering support that respects the individual's autonomy. Here are ways to provide that support:

**Educate Yourself**: Understanding the basics of neurodiversity and the specific needs or experiences of the neurodivergent individuals in your life is the first step toward providing meaningful support.

**Ask, Don't Assume**: Each person's experience of neurodivergence is unique. Asking how you can support them, rather than making assumptions, ensures your efforts are genuinely helpful.

**Advocate Together**: Stand alongside neurodivergent individuals in their advocacy efforts, whether supporting them in meetings, helping to navigate resources, or amplifying their voices in broader advocacy work.

**Fostering an Inclusive Environment**

Inclusivity isn't just about removing barriers; it's about actively creating spaces where neurodivergent individuals can thrive. This inclusivity extends from personal relationships to workplaces, schools, and social settings. Considerations for fostering inclusivity might include:

**Flexible Structures**: From flexible work hours to alternative assignment formats in schools, structuring environments to accommodate various needs can make a profound difference.

**Social Support**: Encourage and facilitate social connections that respect the individual's preferences and comfort levels. This might mean small group interactions rather than large gatherings or clear expectations rather than spontaneous social demands.

**Accessibility of Resources**: Ensure that mental health resources, information, and support services are accessible to neurodivergent individuals, considering communication preferences and sensory needs.

In embracing neurodiversity within mental health strategies, we acknowledge the rich tapestry of human cognition and the importance of honoring each individual's unique mental landscape. Through personalized strategy, advocacy, active support, and fostering inclusive environments, the conversation around mental health becomes more encompassing, more understanding, and deeply enriched by the diversity it seeks to serve.

## 4.11 Overcoming Financial Barriers to Mental Health Care

The path to accessing mental health care is often obstructed by financial hurdles, casting a shadow over the hope of receiving necessary support. The cost of therapy sessions, medication, and even the time away from work can add up, creating a daunting barrier for many. Yet, navigating these financial challenges is crucial for ensuring that mental health care is within reach for all who need it.

### Facing the Financial Challenge

The reality of financial barriers to accessing mental health care cannot be understated. For countless individuals, the prospect of affording regular therapy sessions or psychiatric evaluations seems like a distant dream. The stress of managing these expenses, on top of existing mental health struggles, can exacerbate feelings of helplessness and despair. Recognizing this issue is the first step towards finding solutions that bridge the gap between need and access.

### Low-cost and Free Resources

Thankfully, a range of low-cost and even free mental health resources are available for those who find traditional therapy routes financially prohibitive:

Community Mental Health Centers often offer sliding-scale fees based on income, making therapy more affordable.

Online Platforms provide access to licensed therapists at reduced rates, and some even offer a set number of free sessions.

University Clinics often have mental health services open to the public, provided by graduate students under professional supervision, at low costs.

Support Groups, both in-person and online, offer a space for sharing experiences and coping strategies without the price tag of one-on-one therapy.

**Insurance and Assistance Programs**

Navigating the labyrinth of insurance coverage for mental health services can be overwhelming, yet understanding your policy details can unlock access to subsidized care:

**Review Your Policy**: Take the time to understand what mental health services your insurance covers, including the number of therapy sessions and any preferred providers.

**Medicaid and Medicare**: These government programs can provide comprehensive mental health coverage for those eligible.

**Employee Assistance Programs (EAPs)**: Many employers offer EAPs that provide short-term counseling and referral services at no cost to the employee.

**Advocacy for Affordable Care**

While individual efforts to find affordable care are crucial, collective action toward systemic change holds the power to dismantle financial barriers on a larger scale. Engaging in advocacy for more accessible mental health care can involve:

Petitioning for Legislation that mandates comprehensive mental health coverage in all insurance plans.

Supporting Non-Profit Organizations that work towards making mental health care more affordable and accessible.

Raising Awareness about the importance of mental health care and the need for financial barriers to be removed.

The financial aspect of accessing mental health care presents a significant challenge, yet it can be navigated with the correct information and resources. From exploring low-cost options and understanding insurance coverage to engaging in advocacy efforts, paths forward lead to support without the burden of financial strain.

## 4.12 Keeping Motivation Alive in Your Mental Health Journey

Motivation acts as the wind beneath the wings of our mental health endeavors. It propels us forward, even through the harshest storms, guiding us towards a haven of well-being. Yet, maintaining this momentum can sometimes feel like trying to light a fire in the pouring rain. It requires understanding its essence, identifying the dampeners, and knowing how to kindle it, keeping the flame alive against all odds.

### The Role of Motivation

Motivation is the driving force that initiates and sustains our actions toward achieving mental health improvements. It gets us out of bed in the morning to meditate, encourages us to reach out to a therapist, and pushes us to engage in activities that nourish our souls. Without it, our desires for better mental health remain just that—desires, untransformed into action.

### Overcoming Motivational Barriers

Several obstacles can hinder our journey to maintain motivation, acting like gusts of wind that threaten to extinguish our flame:

**Lack of Immediate Results**: The journey to improved mental health often shows its rewards only in the long run, discouraging those seeking quick fixes.

**Overwhelming Goals**: Setting too ambitious goals can lead to frustration and a sense of defeat when they're not met.

**Self-Doubt**: Doubting our ability to change can sap our motivation, making every step feel heavier than the last.

**Strategies to navigate these barriers include:**

**Adjusting Expectations**: Recognize and accept that progress in mental health is gradual and celebrate the small victories along the way.

**Breaking Down Goals**: Divide larger objectives into smaller, manageable tasks that provide a more straightforward path forward and a sense of achievement.

**Affirming Self-Belief**: Engage in positive self-talk and remind yourself of past successes, however small, to bolster your belief in your ability to overcome challenges.

**Setting and Celebrating Milestones**

Milestones mark the journey to improved mental health, each representing a step closer to our goal. Setting these milestones:

Provides a roadmap that guides our efforts, offering clear markers of progress.

Allows for adjustment of strategies based on what's working and what's not.

Celebrating these milestones is equally crucial. It reinforces the positive behavior that led there and boosts our motivation to continue. This could be as simple as acknowledging a week of consistent meditation or recognizing the courage it took to attend a therapy session.

### Long-term Vision

Keeping a long-term vision in focus can help steer us through the ebbs and flows of motivation. This vision:

It serves as a reminder of why we started this journey, anchoring us during times of doubt or stagnation.

It encourages us to look beyond the immediate challenges and keep our eyes on the broader horizon of improved well-being.

Visualizing positive outcomes—imagining a future where we're thriving, not just surviving—can be a powerful motivator. Setting overarching goals that align with this vision ensures that every step feels meaningful and directed, no matter how small.

In essence, motivation in our mental health journey is both the starting point and the fuel that keeps us moving forward. It requires nurturing, through understanding its role, confronting the barriers with strategic action, setting and celebrating milestones, and always keeping our long-term vision in sight. With each step, we weave a stronger, more resilient fabric of mental well-being, enriched by our continued efforts and the lessons learned along the way.

As we close this chapter, we reflect on the intricate dance of maintaining motivation—understanding its nature, facing challenges head-on, and always moving toward our envisioned future. This journey, with its ups and downs, teaches us the value of perseverance, the importance of small victories, and the power of a long-term vision. As we turn the page, we carry with us the knowledge that, in pursuing mental health, our motivation is both our compass and our anchor, guiding us toward a horizon of hope and healing.

# References

Is Information Overload Hurting Mental Health?
https://www.psychologytoday.com/us/blog/denying-the-grave/202006/is-information-overload-hurting-mental-health

Digital Detox: What to Know
https://www.webmd.com/balance/what-is-digital-detox

How well is telepsychology working?
https://www.apa.org/monitor/2020/07/cover-telepsychology

Some of the best online support groups
https://www.medicalnewstoday.com/articles/online-support-groups

What are the benefits of mindfulness?
https://www.apa.org/monitor/2012/07-08/ce-corner

undefined undefined

30 Grounding Techniques to Quiet Distressing Thoughts
https://www.healthline.com/health/grounding-techniques

Effectiveness of physical activity interventions for improving ...
https://bjsm.bmj.com/content/57/18/1203#:~:text=Results%20showed%20that%20physical%20activity,usual%20care%20across%20all%20populations.

What are the benefits of mindfulness?
https://www.apa.org/monitor/2012/07-08/ce-corner

Online self-help CBT techniques - Every Mind Matters
https://www.nhs.uk/every-mind-matters/mental-wellbeing-tips/self-help-cbt-techniques/

Nutritional psychiatry: Your brain on food
https://www.health.harvard.edu/blog/nutritional-psychiatry-your-brain-on-food-201511168626

Resilience: Build skills to endure hardship - Mayo Clinic
https://www.mayoclinic.org/tests-procedures/resilience-training/in-depth/resilience/art-20046311

Effectiveness of school-based mental health programs on ...
https://www.ncbi.nlm.nih.gov/pmc/articles/PMC7377131/

Loneliness and Social Isolation — Tips for Staying Connected
https://www.nia.nih.gov/health/loneliness-and-social-isolation/loneliness-and-social-isolation-tips-staying-connected

Overcoming stigmas, barriers to mental health care
https://www.mayoclinichealthsystem.org/hometown-health/speaking-of-health/overcoming-mental-health-care-barriers

Success Stories | instituteofliving.org | Institute of Living
https://instituteofliving.org/health-wellness/health-resources/success-stories

Made in the USA
Monee, IL
16 April 2024

dcb1aa75-bfc9-40d0-bfee-c29091f60839R01